"*Seek the Living God* provides an individualized formation path for each inquirer leading them to lifelong discipleship. Using five insightful questions to engage each seeker's unique needs, the evidence of their ongoing conversion is illuminated through dialogue with an RCIA team mentor. A model calendar, formation plan, and creative involvement with community provide a flexible guide suited to diverse parish RCIA teams."

> — Emily Filippi
> Director of Office of Christian Formation
> Diocese of Richmond

"*Seek the Living God* is a creative and practical resource for those who lead the Period of the Precatechumenate (Inquiry) in the RCIA. Nick Wagner shares great insight and experience as he breaks open this important time of evangelization. He provides extremely helpful questions, examples, tools, and ideas for the period of inquiry, which all too often looks like 'Catholic classes' rather than a time of encountering the living God, hearing the Good News of Jesus Christ, and opening one's life to the power of the Holy Spirit. This book will help RCIA leaders and teams to avoid the temptation of a 'one size fits all' precatechumenate, and will enable them to recognize and bring out the many hues of those who seek the living God."

> — Karen Kane
> Director of the Office for Divine Worship and Sacraments
> Archdiocese of Cincinnati

# Seek the Living God

Five RCIA Inquiry Questions for Making Disciples

*Nick Wagner*

**LITURGICAL PRESS**

Collegeville, Minnesota

www.litpress.org

1     2     3     4     5     6     7     8     9

**Library of Congress Cataloging-in-Publication Data**

Names: Wagner, Nick, 1957– author.
Title: Seek the living God : five RCIA inquiry questions for making disciples / Nick Wagner.
Description: Collegeville, Minnesota : Liturgical Press, 2017. | Series: TeamRCIA | Includes bibliographical references.
Identifiers: LCCN 2017041124 (print) | LCCN 2017020309 (ebook) | ISBN 9780814645406 (ebook) | ISBN 9780814645161
Subjects: LCSH: Catechetics—Catholic Church. | Questioning. | Discipling (Christianity) | Initiation rites—Religious aspects—Catholic Church—Study and teaching.
Classification: LCC BX930 (print) | LCC BX930 .W28 2017 (ebook) | DDC 268/.82—dc23
LC record available at https://lccn.loc.gov/2017041124

# Contents

Introduction   1

*Chapter 1*
The Purpose of Inquiry   13

*Chapter 2*
Adapting Contract Learning for Faith Formation
and Conversion   22

*Chapter 3*
The First Question: *Where Have You Been?*   28

*Chapter 4*
The Second Question: *Where Are You Now?*   35

*Chapter 5*
The Third Question: *Where Do You Want to Get To?*   40

*Chapter 6*
The Fourth Question:
*How Are You Going to Get to Where You Want to Go?*   50

*Chapter 7*
The Fifth Question:
*How Will You Know You Have Arrived?*   56

*Chapter 8*
Creating a Faith Formation Plan   60

*Chapter 9*
Implementing the Plan   66

*Chapter 10*
Discernment for Readiness   78

*Chapter 11*
The Ideal Catechist   83

*Conclusion*
What Could Happen?   90

*Appendix 1*
A Model Calendar for a Formation Plan for Seekers   97

*Appendix 2*
Goal-Setting Worksheet for Becoming a Disciple   109

*Appendix 3*
Catholic Prayers   111

Bibliography   123

# Introduction

Some time ago, I found myself in a new parish, and I volunteered to join the RCIA team. At my first team meeting, the discussion was about who would teach which topic for the precatechumenate classes in the fall. There were ten classes on the schedule that covered things like "The Existence of God," "Jesus," "Holy Spirit and Trinity," "The Church," and so on.

The inquirers would all be given textbooks that contained all the topics, and they were expected to read the appropriate chapter before class. The classes met every Monday evening for 90 minutes from September through November.

On the Sunday after the last class, the inquirers would all come to Mass to celebrate the combined Rite of Acceptance into the Order of Catechumens and Rite of Welcoming Baptized Candidates.

I was told that this schedule and process were the same every year, year in and year out. It didn't matter who the inquirers were. Anyone who wanted to become Catholic was expected to attend the same ten classes that started every year in mid-September. (And that was just the precatechumenate! They still had to attend all the classes during the catechumenate period.)

If someone asked about becoming Catholic in January or May or August, he or she was told that classes start in September.

I want to tell you about four of the inquirers I met that year.

## Four Seekers

Bill was an evangelical Protestant. He had read the Bible cover to cover and could quote a seemingly unlimited number of passages in response to any situation or question he was faced with. His deep spirituality and prayer life led him to seek a deeper experience of faith that he hoped he would find in the Catholic Church. As part of his search, Bill had visited most of the parishes in the diocese and had had personal conversations with more than twenty-five priests.

Kevin was an ex-convict and a recovering addict. He had prison tattoos up and down both arms. He had been raised in a Catholic family but had never been baptized. When I met him, he had been married to a faithful Catholic woman for six years and had been going to Mass with her all that time.

Adhi had been raised as a nominal Buddhist, but his family was not active in their religion. Adhi caused a bit of a problem for the team because he showed up three weeks after the precatechumenate classes had begun. There was a lot of conversation about letting him join the existing group of seekers and trying to catch him up or making him wait until classes started again the next year.

The fourth inquirer was Alice. Alice was not really an "inquirer." Alice didn't believe in God and didn't intend to become Catholic. She was engaged to one of our parishioners, and because she was in love with him, she had agreed to get married at our church. She also would occasionally come to Mass with her fiancé. But she had no intention of signing up for Catholic classes.

At this point, I felt like the guy who was warned about the hazards of drinking. He had been told that vodka over ice would give him kidney failure, rum and ice would cause liver failure, and whiskey with ice would give him heart problems. The solution, he was told, was to avoid ice.

The RCIA team was focused on the ice, and the ice was not the problem. Each of the four inquirers I met had specific needs, all of which were different from each other's. But nobody was talking about that.

## What Do People Need?

You have probably heard of Maslow's hierarchy of needs. In 1943, psychologist Abraham Maslow identified a pyramid of human needs ("A Theory of Human Motivation," *Psychological Review*). The most basic, physical needs (such as food and water), are at the bottom. The highest, creative and spiritual needs (the desire to become the best you can be or "self-actualization"), are at the top. According to Maslow's theory, needs higher on the pyramid cannot be met unless the needs below them have been met. If you are starving, for example, you aren't too worried about being a good swimmer or a fast reader.

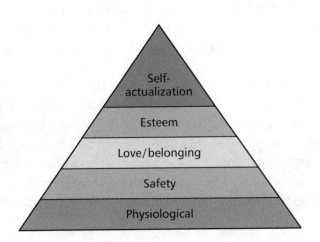

Usually (although not always), seekers who come to us are not lacking for physical needs or safety needs. Some seekers who come to us are looking to satisfy the third level of need: love and belonging. They are looking for friendship, intimacy, or a sense of family.

Other seekers are at the fourth level of need: esteem. If someone has low self-esteem, that person may be seeking respect, validation, and acceptance.

In Maslow's original theory, the highest level of need is self-actualization. Some seekers come to us wishing to become the model Christian, or an ideal parent, or more spiritually disciplined.

In his later years, Maslow added a sixth level: self-transcendence. He came to believe that a fully actualized human is one who has some higher goal outside oneself, an altruistic personality focused on the good of others. (See "Critique of Self-Actualization Theory," in *Future Visions: The Unpublished Papers of Abraham Maslow.*)

It is helpful for RCIA teams to have an understanding of Maslow's hierarchy, but it is not a perfect system. Maslow himself said there are no rigid boundaries between the levels. There can be significant overlap among the various kinds of needs. And later researchers have criticized Maslow's theory as either being completely inadequate for describing human need or as being too culturally specific.

The important takeaway for RCIA teams is that every seeker who comes to us will have a unique set of needs and a hierarchy of needs. The hierarchy may not match Maslow's, but it is there. If someone asks us what they have to do to become Catholic, and we have one single answer for everyone who asks, we are almost sure to miss meeting the true needs of almost everyone. We are focusing on the "ice" and not on the unique circumstances of each seeker.

## The RCIA Team

There were seven people on that RCIA team, not counting myself. All of them were good souls, dedicated volunteers who truly wanted to help people seeking to become Catholic. They had never been formally trained in the catechumenate process. They didn't even know there was an official text and Rite.

Even so, they had a lot of gifts. They were compassionate, caring, and concerned about the inquirers. They sacrificed hours and hours of their time to plan and execute not only the precatechumenate classes but also classes for the catechumenate and mystagogy periods. They were giving and loving folks who were doing the best they could.

My challenge was to find a way to help them channel their gifts, energy, and commitment in a way that would be truly helpful to the inquirers. The team, of course, already believed they were being helpful. They believed in God and Jesus and the Spirit and the church. They knew in their hearts that if they could teach others about those things, the inquirers would come to believe as they believed. But that way of thinking is still focusing on "the ice." It reduces every seeker's need to a pat set of answers that must serve every situation. It is a one-size-fits-all approach that is rarely successful in leading inquirers to a lasting faith.

I am not sure how that RCIA team developed their approach to formation. If I had to guess, I might say that each of them was asked to be on the RCIA team by either the pastor or another team member. I would guess that most of them protested they didn't "know enough" to be helpful. And then, perhaps, some gentle Catholic guilt was applied along with a promise that "everything you need is in the textbook we use." It's easy enough to find such textbooks. Other teams find class outlines on the internet. Some even use prerecorded videos so all the RCIA team has to do is turn on the television.

Textbooks and videos might be helpful in some catechetical settings. But for most inquirers, these kinds of resources are responding to the wrong level of need. An inquirer is someone who is seeking. When we meet them, often they tell us that what they are seeking is to "become Catholic." But becoming Catholic means one thing to Bill and another to Kevin and another to Adhi. And Alice wasn't even seeking to "become Catholic," but she was, indeed, seeking something. The challenge for RCIA teams is to discover the exact need for each seeker.

## How Do We Know What Each Inquirer Is Seeking?

Coincidentally, about the same time I was getting to know my new RCIA team, I also came across two books by adult educator

Malcolm S. Knowles: *The Adult Learner: A Neglected Species* and *Using Learning Contracts.*

In *The Adult Learner*, Knowles wrote:

> The most effective facilitator is one who can encourage adults to consider rationally and carefully perspectives and interpretations of the world that diverge from those they already hold. (99)

This seemed to me to be exactly the goal of an RCIA team in relation to an inquirer. Knowles lists seven things that successful adult educators do:

1. Prepare a conducive learning environment.

2. Create a tool for mutual planning.

3. Diagnose learning needs.

4. Formulate a plan to meet those needs.

5. Design the learning experience.

6. Facilitate the learning experience with suitable techniques and materials.

7. Evaluate the outcomes (see *The Adult Learner*, 120).

Knowles expanded on that seven-point process in *Using Learning Contracts.* In his preface, he wrote,

> The one [technique] that has made the most difference in what I do and has solved the most problems that have plagued me as an educator is the process of contract learning. (xi)

Contract learning is difficult to define because it can take on a variety of forms. Indeed, in *Using Learning Contracts*, Knowles lists "religious institutions" as one of the many places contract learning is used. Most of his examples, however, are better suited to academia and business training.

Even so, by studying his examples and understanding the underlying principles of contract learning, it is possible to apply

Knowles's insights to adult faith formation. Knowles asks and answers the question of how to develop a learning contract:

> There is no one right way. In fact, one of the chief virtues of contract learning is its almost infinite flexibility. Its heart is the process of negotiation between learners, facilitators, and resource persons. (43)

I took his message to heart and set out to adapt the principles of contract learning to developing a faith formation plan for inquirers. Contract learning offers an effective and powerful listening tool. And the contract learning process also provides a clear map of the unique formation process that will be most effective for each inquirer.

---

### Malcolm Knowles's six assumptions of adult learning

1. **Need to know:** Adults need to know the reason for learning something.

2. **Self-concept:** Adults need to be responsible for their decisions on education; involvement in the planning and evaluation of their instruction.

3. **Experience:** The learner's experience (including error) provides the basis for learning activities.

4. **Readiness:** Adults are most interested in learning subjects having immediate relevance to their work and/or personal lives.

5. **Orientation:** Adult learning is problem-centered rather than content-oriented.

6. **Motivation:** Adults respond better to internal versus external motivators.

Source: *The Adult Learner: A Neglected Species*, 57–63.

# Seek the Living God

The purpose of this book is to give RCIA teams a way out of the one-size-fits-all precatechumenate process so many of us have fallen into. In these pages, you will discover the true purpose of the precatechumenate period and how to use this important time to discover what the inquirers are actually seeking.

The first paragraph of the *Rite of Christian Initiation of Adults* gets at the core of what all of us are actually seeking. In identifying the purpose of the initiation process, the rite says:

> The rite of Christian initiation presented here is designed for adults who, after hearing the mystery of Christ proclaimed, consciously and freely *seek the living God* and enter the way of faith and conversion as the Holy Spirit opens their hearts. (1, emphasis added)

Underneath every request to "become Catholic" is a deep, heartfelt longing for God. Your mission, as a guide in the initiation process, is to help seekers explore that longing and to enter fully on "the way of faith and conversion."

This book will give you the skills you need to start your inquirers on a path to lifelong discipleship by listening deeply to their true needs. You will be confident that you are leading your seekers through a fruitful, conversion-centered inquiry process that will set them on a clear path to living and praying as committed Catholics.

After just a few meetings with your seekers, you will be able to easily create a customized faith formation plan that is tailored to the unique needs of each person. And the best part is that the seekers do most of the work in developing their own plan. Your role shifts from being the Catholic "expert" to being a mentor and coach.

And once you understand how the five-question process works, you can easily train others to use it. New team members don't have to worry about "knowing enough" to be on the team. They just have to be able to ask five questions.

Before we get to the five questions, we will take a fresh look at the purpose of the precatechumenate period of the *Rite of Christian Initiation of Adults*. These five questions are ideally used during the inquiry phase of initiation. However, many RCIA teams have been using the precatechumenate as a kind of "mini-course" or introduction to Catholic teaching. If initiation is going to be a true conversion process, we have to recover a more authentic understanding of the precatechumenate. That's what we will do in chapter 1.

Next, in chapter 2, we will examine adult learning theory, specifically in regard to establishing initial goals and processes for learning. For adults to learn effectively, they have to take responsibility for their own formation. And catechists have to let go of the need to "teach." If we can make this shift in our understanding of the learning process, our initiation processes will flourish.

Chapters 3 through 7 cover the actual questions we will use in the inquiry process. It is helpful to think of these five questions more as categories than literal questions. To help with that understanding, each of these chapters begins with twenty different ways to ask the same question. In addition, I provide three examples of ways you might ask each question when talking with children and their families. I encourage you to use all of these examples as inspiration for your own questions that best fit you and your inquirers.

In chapter 8, I show you, step by step, how to shape the responses you received to the five questions into a practical, workable, customized faith formation plan for each inquirer. The power of this process is that each formation plan springs from the actual wants and needs of the individual seeker. Because each plan is specific to each seeker, you will see a much greater commitment to lifelong discipleship in your seekers.

Chapter 9 gives you a clear and concise guide for implementing your seekers' faith formation plans. In this chapter, I show you how to take seriously that directive that "the initiation of adults is the responsibility of all the baptized" (RCIA 9). This process will only work if we move the formation of the seekers out of the classroom and into the active life of your parish. In a sense, your entire parish becomes your "RCIA team," and you become more of a facilitator to help the parish live out "its apostolic vocation to give help to those who are searching for Christ" (RCIA 9).

One of the most frequent questions I receive when I talk with RCIA teams is: How do we know when the seeker is ready? There are both objective and subjective criteria we can use to answer that question. One of the stronger points of this formation process, however, is that the seekers themselves will establish their own markers for readiness. This is such a game changer! We no longer have to be the gatekeepers of the sacraments. In a collaborative discernment process with each seeker and under the guidance of the Holy Spirit, the weight of the decision for readiness moves off of our shoulders and onto the heart of each seeker.

For many RCIA leaders, this way of implementing faith formation will require new ways of thinking and new skills. Even so, I believe that most of us who are passionate about the catechumenate process have within us all the gifts we need to be able to evolve into this new way of doing things. So in chapter 11, I spend some time discussing the "ideal catechist." None of us has all the skills and talents we need to do this ministry perfectly. But all of us have exactly the gifts the Holy Spirit has given us to accomplish the mission to which we have been called. My hope is this description of the ideal will help all of us to stretch ourselves to be the best catechists we can be for the sake of the seekers.

The concluding chapter is a question for ourselves: What could happen if we did this? In building relationships and engaging the larger community, the question is more important than the answer. If we want to form committed disciples, we have to ask the right question. If we want to involve the entire parish, we have to ask the right question. And if we want to become the best catechists that God has called us to be, we have to ask ourselves the right question.

I have also provided a few helpful resources at the end of the book. There is a bibliography of resources for those of you who wish to dive deep into understanding this learning process. There is also a model calendar that provides a sample formation plan for seekers. Another helpful resource is a goal-setting worksheet for your seekers to use. And finally, an extensive collection of Catholic prayers you can use with your seekers in the initial inquiry process and throughout their formation.

The core of this process is very simple, and you can use these questions with your very next inquirer. You will be amazed at the powerful conversion that will happen with your inquirers—and with you. So let's get started.

*Chapter* 1

# The Purpose of Inquiry

In academia, we might start the contract learning process by identifying the objective of a course of study. In an evangelization and conversion process, we begin by asking where the Holy Spirit is leading the inquirer.

We will do that by asking the inquirers five questions. Before we get to the questions, however, we have to all get on the same page about the purpose of inquiry.

RCIA teams will often say that the most difficult part of the RCIA process to implement is the period of mystagogy. I must respectfully disagree. The period that RCIA teams seem to have the most trouble with is the first period. All of the difficulties we have with the period of mystagogy are usually caused by the way we implement the period of precatechumenate.

Someone told me recently the precatechumenate in their parish is one session. One parish I was in had a ten-session precatechumenate program that required a textbook. If you Google "precatechumenate," you can find precatechumenate "lesson plans." You can also find YouTube videos that seem intended for inquirers to watch as the core element of their precatechumenate process.

All of these are misunderstandings of the purpose of this first period of the RCIA process. If you turn to the "Outline for Christian Initiation of Adults" (just before paragraph 36 of the RCIA), we see there that the precatechumenate "is a time of no fixed duration or structure."

Furthermore, RCIA 36 says the precatechumenate "is a time for evangelization." Indeed, we sometimes forget that the official title for this period is "Period of Evangelization and Precatechumenate." If we focus on the first part of the title, *evangelization*, how can we conceive of a set number of sessions, lesson plans, and videos as the core of this period? Evangelization is (or should be) happening all the time. If we are truly evangelizing, we can never tell inquirers to "come back when classes start."

People keep usurping the word *evangelization*, making it more difficult for us to accomplish the primary mission of the RCIA—go and make disciples. First it was the evangelicals, who used the word to identify a portion of Christianity quite distinct from Catholicism. On the face of it, there's nothing wrong with a group defining itself with the term *evangelization*. The difficulty for Catholics, however, has been our reluctance to speak and act as evangelists for fear of becoming identified with some of the more fundamentalist and flamboyant types of evangelicals.

Next it was businesses, especially in the tech industry. Guy Kawasaki, a former Apple employee originally responsible for marketing the Macintosh in 1984, initiated the idea of the evangelization of a product or business. His goal was to create passionate user-advocates ("product evangelists") for the Macintosh and the Apple brand. His goal was the same as ours, just translated for business. We strive to bring the good news of Jesus Christ to the world. He was bringing what he saw as the good news about the Apple brand to the world.

## Catholic Evangelization

If we are going to be effective evangelizers, we have to understand what Catholics mean by *evangelization*.

The reason we exist as a church is to evangelize. In Matthew's gospel, the last thing Jesus said to his followers was: "Go, therefore, and make disciples of all nations" (28:19).

Pope Paul VI wrote: "The task of evangelizing all people constitutes the essential mission of the Church. . . . She exists in order to evangelize" (On Evangelization in the Modern World, 14).

And Pope Francis said: "All the baptized, whatever their position in the Church or their level of instruction in the faith, are agents of evangelization. . . . Every Christian is challenged, here and now, to be actively engaged in evangelization" (Joy of the Gospel, 120).

Sometimes I read churchy pronouncements like these, and I get the same feeling I get when I have to go to the dentist. I know I should. It's good for me. But it's going to be pretty uncomfortable, and I don't really want to.

Pope Francis asks us to think about evangelization a little more deeply. He reminds us that all of us, at some point, were lost. We were hurting. Maybe we were hopeless. And in the midst of our despair, Jesus reached out to us and saved us. Maybe Jesus came to us through a friend or a family member. Maybe in a moment of prayer or at Mass. Maybe in some "coincidence" that reminded us that God is always with us. In whatever way, Jesus rescued us.

Today, right now, there are millions of people who don't know that saving love. They are falling deeper and deeper into hopelessness and despair. And all of us who have felt the love of Jesus know that we don't have to suffer any longer. Pope Francis said the church is a field hospital on a battlefield and our number-one job is to heal the wounds (see Spadaro, "A Big Heart Open to God," *America*).

## What If?

If we think of evangelization as healing wounds, that sounds a lot more Catholic. We don't have to walk up to strangers and ask them if they are saved. We don't have to quote long passages from the Bible. We don't even have to know much theology. We

---

## New evangelization

Where does "new evangelization" fit into the church's mission to evangelize? Pope John Paul II promoted the need for a "new evangelization" or a "re-evangelization" of Catholics and other Christians who "have lost a living sense of the faith, or even no longer consider themselves members of the Church" (see Mission of the Redeemer, 33).

Pope Francis affirmed the need for a new evangelization, noting that it is carried out in three principal ways:

1. In the area of ordinary pastoral ministry, especially Sunday worship, by which the faithful are nourished and renewed

2. In the area of ministry to baptized members who have let their faith grow cold and who need a commitment to the Gospel

3. In the area of those who do not know Christ or who have always rejected him.

About this third area, Pope Francis says: "Lastly, we cannot forget that evangelization is first and foremost about preaching the Gospel to *those who do not know Jesus Christ or who have always rejected him* (Joy of the Gospel, 14).

The place of new evangelization—the restoration of the lapsed baptized to a life of discipleship—is at the service of primary evangelization—the announcement of Jesus Christ to those who have yet to hear the Good News.

---

just have to know the love of Jesus and be willing to love those who need love.

Pope Francis also said that, like the woman at the well who evangelized her entire town after one conversation with Jesus:

"Anyone who has truly experienced God's saving love does not need much time or lengthy training to go out and proclaim that love" (Joy of the Gospel, 120).

## Three Movements of Evangelization

As Catholics, we are not known for our evangelization skills. We tend to be quiet about our faith, careful not to offend or make others feel awkward. We absolutely love the meme, "Preach the gospel at all times, and when necessary, use words." That notion seemingly lets us off the hook about talking about our faith. Can't we just live by example and let that serve as our evangelization?

In part, yes, we can. Pope Paul VI said that our proclamation of the Good News is first of all a "wordless witness" by which the actions of our lives "stir up irresistible questions" in the hearts of others (see On Evangelization in the Modern World, 21).

What we are currently doing, however, is not working. Our wordless witness is not enough. We need to be able to explain why we do what we do—"what Peter called always having 'your answer ready for people who ask you the reason for the hope that you all have'" (1 Pet 3:15, qtd. in On Evangelization in the Modern World, 22). Pope Paul VI said:

> The Good News proclaimed by the witness of life sooner or later has to be proclaimed by the word of life. There is no true evangelization if the name, the teaching, the life, the promises, the kingdom and the mystery of Jesus of Nazareth, the Son of God, are not proclaimed. (22)

The third movement of evangelization is when the message "is listened to, accepted, and assimilated, and when it arouses a genuine adherence in the one who has thus received it" (23). It is at this third movement that most RCIA teams are formally engaged in evangelization. We usually meet seekers once they have already encountered Christ on some level, and they come to us with a desire to know more.

# How to evangelize like a Catholic

Most of us are not going to start quoting Scripture and inviting strangers into a personal relationship with Jesus. However, there are some simple, gentle ways we can put words to our "wordless witness." Here are a few ideas.

1. Change your perception of yourself. Instead of identifying yourself as an RCIA team member, think of yourself as someone who shares faith with others. For example, if asked, "What do you do in your parish?" reply: "Primarily, I share my faith, and I help others grow in faith." Even if you can't bring yourself to say that out loud, think it to yourself before you reply.

2. Pray every morning that the Holy Spirit will give you a chance to share your faith with someone.

3. Talk to strangers. Talk to people at the grocery store, the coffee shop, on the bus or subway, or at a restaurant. Set a goal for three, four, or five conversations a day with strangers.

4. Talk about everyday life. You don't have to begin the conversation with a deep religious question. Use Jesus as your model. He didn't walk up to the woman at the well and begin by asking her about her faith life and her many husbands. He asked for a drink of water. Just ask for a drink. Or comment on the weather. Or what you had for dessert. Or the latest victory of your home team. Just start things off, and see where the conversation goes.

5. If it feels right, ask a deeper question. Don't force the conversation to a deeper level, but don't shy away from it either. What's the worst that could happen? Here are a few example questions, but come up with your own that fit your personality and interests:

    • How are you growing personally?

- What single thing would you like to make absolutely certain you do (if at all possible) during your lifetime?
- How do you think a person can keep from becoming a workaholic?
- What do you consider to be two major turning points in your life?
- What is something you consider to be a great personal success? Why was it so significant?
- What is the key to maintaining balance in your life?

6. After you ask a question, just listen. Try to hear the answer beneath the answer. Pope Francis says our job is to bind up the wounds. Listen for the wound. You don't have to do anything about the wound right now. Just deeply listening is a healing action.

7. *If it feels right*, offer to pray either with or for the person about what they shared with you. Again, don't force prayer upon people who aren't open to it, but don't automatically assume they aren't interested in your prayer, even if they said they aren't religious. Let the Holy Spirit guide you.

8. *If it feels right*, invite the person to join you at church this coming Sunday.

## When Does Evangelization "Start"?

What this means for RCIA teams is that we are *always* in the first period of the RCIA—the period of evangelization and precatechumenate. It doesn't start in September. It doesn't end after one session or ten sessions. And it's not about teaching theology. Evangelization is about healing the wounds.

When an inquirer comes to us and asks "How do I become Catholic?" there is almost always something deeper under that question. If we don't take the time to listen to the deeper questions, we will miss the opportunity to heal the wounds.

If we are going to be effective at this, we have to rethink how we encounter each inquirer. When someone walks into the church office, calls, emails, or speaks to you after Mass about becoming Catholic, what would be the most loving way to encounter that person who may be suffering?

If we were medics in a field hospital, our first response would be to drop everything and attend to the wounded. Then we would start binding up the wound right there on the battlefield. We wouldn't wait. We'd start right away.

So ask yourself, in your situation, in your parish, how can all of your "medics"—your RCIA team, your pastor, your parish secretary, and everyone in your parish—develop a more immediate loving response to inquirers?

The next thing to do is a fuller diagnosis. You want to find out what the deeper wounds are.

And, finally, you want to treat the wounds with a healing therapy designed specifically for each person.

In order to diagnose and treat the deeper wounds, we are going to create a faith formation plan using an adapted contract learning process. To develop a specific faith formation plan for each inquirer, we will focus on five general questions.

These five questions are much more than just questions, however. They are invitations to tell stories. And in the stories, we will learn how the Holy Spirit has already been working in the heart of each inquirer. We will learn the unique call each inquirer has heard. And we will discern the best path forward to help each inquirer encounter the saving love of Jesus.

At the end of this five-question process, we will have a clear faith formation plan, designed specifically for each inquirer. We will have ongoing measures to determine the progress each inquirer is making toward his or her healing process. And we will have observable criteria that will be clear to both the inquirer and the RCIA team about the readiness of each inquirer to take on the next steps in becoming disciples.

Before we get to the questions, let's take a deeper look at how the contract learning process can be adapted for faith formation and conversion.

*Chapter* 2

# Adapting Contract Learning for Faith Formation and Conversion

Many years ago, I began to be uncomfortable with the way I was handling the precatechumenate process. I had long since abandoned the notion that the precatechumenate was a time for introductory lessons. But what I was doing instead didn't seem satisfactory. I met with seekers a few times and, based mostly on gut-feeling, I decided if and how they should enter the formation process. Too much of the precatechumenate depended upon me and my own discernment of the movement of the Holy Spirit. But the Spirit was moving primarily in the hearts of the seekers. I struggled with how I could get better at helping people discern the action of the Spirit in their own lives—some of whom had never heard the term *Holy Spirit*.

That's when I came across the idea of contract learning developed by Malcolm Knowles. I was so excited by what I was reading that I tried out some of his ideas on the very next seeker I encountered.

Joe was nineteen years old when I met him. He was a barely active Catholic, coming to Mass once or twice a month. He had skipped confirmation when he was in high school. After graduating, he started working full-time. His transition into adulthood was rocky. He still lived with his mother and younger siblings, and life at home was tense. His work environment was also strained. Joe thought getting confirmed and becoming more active in his faith might bring him peace.

Honestly, Joe was Catholic enough that he probably would have found a spiritual path without my help. He had a deep faith. His main problem was that he was young and had not yet learned how to develop his childhood faith into his new adult circumstances. Even so, I was excited to help him if I could, and I was determined to bring my new understanding of adult learning to the process.

I have to say I was horrible. I stuck too closely to Knowles's format, which was designed to get college students more deeply engaged in their academic classes. Some of my questions to Joe just didn't make sense. But wow! Even with my inept use of the structure, it was clear that I was onto something. I had never had the depth of conversation that I had with Joe at such an initial stage of the formation process. I was used to waiting weeks, even months for seekers to open up and show me their deep needs. Joe and I were deep into spiritual exploration within ten minutes.

Since then, I've never looked back. Now I use an adapted version of Knowles's contract learning process with every seeker I encounter. I use the process with prospective team members. I use it with sponsors. The questions serve as a structure for discovering how the Holy Spirit is guiding us. And being more deeply attuned to the Spirit, in turn, leads to deeper, more effective conversion.

As I mentioned, Malcolm Knowles's descriptions of contract learning seem to be derived from classroom or business settings. I have made several adaptations to his model to make it more appropriate for developing a faith formation plan.

## Language

I don't use the language of academia or business to describe this process. So instead of constructing a learning contract, we are developing a faith formation plan. Instead of talking about competencies, we talk about gifts (or gifts of the Holy Spirit). Instead of talking about learning, we talk about developing or strengthening our gifts. In this faith formation model, there are no teachers, consultants, or counselors. Instead, our team consists of catechists, mentors, sponsors, and companions. Also, there are no students. We encounter seekers or inquirers. In the precatechumenate, there are no classes. We have meetings, sessions, dinner, or coffee.

## Process

Knowles's contract learning process most often places the responsibility of creating the contract on the learner. In a college setting, for example, a group of students might attend a lecture on how to construct a learning contract, and then they would be sent off to write a draft. That won't work for us because we are not teaching students. We are developing a relationship with a companion on the journey of seeking God. So our process is going to look and feel a lot more like two friends getting to know one another.

## Environment

If we want to get to know a new friend, we don't ask him or her to fill out a form. We don't meet in a classroom or an office. We don't go over a list of rules and requirements for the friendship. We don't present a schedule of meetings. For this process to be effective, RCIA teams will want to recall the story of Jesus encountering the Samaritan woman at Jacob's well. Jesus definitely had a process and a plan, but his interaction with her was friend-to-friend, not teacher-to-student. For our encounters with seekers today, it would be good for us to identify a "well," a meeting place that seems social and not a business place or classroom.

Also, Jesus didn't take any supplies with him for his encounter. He didn't even have a bucket. Leave all your supplies at home, and just bring yourself to your encounter with the seeker.

## How Many Seekers?

Ideally, you will want to meet one-on-one with a new inquirer. I have sometimes met with two new inquirers together. I don't think the process would work very well if you tried to meet with three or more inquirers at time. If a family is inquiring, that might be different, and you may have an effective process by meeting with everyone together. But for unrelated inquirers, try to meet with them individually. If you don't have enough team members to meet individually with all the inquirers, keep reading.

## Recruit Team Members for Only This Role

Once you understand the five questions, the process itself is very easy to implement. I've trained parishioners to do only this task—meet with new inquirers—just by having them sit in with me as we met with a new seeker. I have found it easy to recruit people for this role because it is time-limited, they can meet in their own homes, and they don't have to know any theology to go through the five questions.

## How Many Meetings?

I do this process in three meetings. At our first gathering, I focus on the first question. (I'll go more deeply into the questions in later chapters.) At the second meeting, we dwell on questions two and three. And at the final meeting, we cover questions four and five.

I imagine that if you did this process over a full day in a retreat-like setting, you could cover all the questions. I've never found a need for that. It has always been easier for the seekers I've met with to find three evenings to meet. How you divide up the questions and the number of meetings is up to you. However, you want to avoid rushing the process. Don't try to cover all five questions in a single evening, for example. Remember, the goal is not to "get done" with the questions. The goal is to develop a relationship with a new friend.

## The Meeting Structure

How you structure the meeting is flexible and depends upon your personality. I always start with prayer. If, for some reason, the seeker is very uncomfortable beginning with prayer, you could skip that. But, of course, at some point I would want to ask him or her about that discomfort. In my experience, however, most seekers might be uncomfortable if I asked them to pray, but they are not at all bothered if I pray.

After prayer, I start right in with the question. The question is really more like a category. So, in the following chapters, I'll give you a lot of different ways to ask similar questions within the same category. Sometimes, questions or answers will overlap the different categories. That's okay. This isn't about getting the categories exactly right. It's about learning about your new friend.

Then I close the meeting with two steps. First, I ask the seeker to go home and write, in journal style, one to three pages about what we talked about. I remind him or her of a few of the questions we talked about, and I ask the seeker to just write down whatever he or she remembers about his or her answers. I also ask the seeker to bring those pages to our next meeting.

The second step is a closing prayer. The opening prayer might be something spontaneous, but the closing prayer is always a traditional prayer. If you think the seeker would be comfortable praying at home, you can also give him or her a copy of the prayer to pray that week. (See appendix 3 for some traditional prayers you can use.)

## Confidentiality

I always assure the seekers that this process is confidential *within a small group*. Whatever they talk about with me or write in the papers they return to me will be shared with the pastor and the RCIA team. But their comments will not go beyond that group.

## Starting Point

The examples of learning contracts Knowles gives in his book all begin with identifying a learning objective. In my adaptation, the identification of a "learning objective" doesn't happen until question three ("Where do you want to get to?"). In a faith formation process, we don't want to start with the learning objective. We believe that the Holy Spirit has been active in the life of the seeker since that person was conceived in the womb. If that's true, we want to know about that person's journey. We want to understand his or her history. So we start with the first question: "Where have you been?"

Chapter 3

# The First Question

## *Where Have You Been?*

Regarding your habits, knowledge, memories, and attitudes about God, where have you been?

### 20 Different Ways to Ask "Where Have You Been?"

1. When did you first become aware of God?

2. Have you ever felt close to God? When did you feel closest?

3. What religion, if any, were you raised in?

4. [If baptized] Describe your baptism. If you were baptized as a baby, what have your family members told you about your baptism? Do you have a baptismal name? Why was that chosen?

5. Create a faith timeline. Indicate the highpoints in your life when you felt God was really close to you.

6. What was your family experience of faith?

7. Did you go to church as a child? As a teenager? As a young adult? How often? What was it like?

8. Have you ever been to a Catholic Mass? What was that like for you?

9. Have you been to any other kind of religious service? What was that like for you?

10. Describe your formal or informal religious education background.

11. Did you have any spiritual heroes as a child? As a teenager? As a young adult?

12. Describe your background and knowledge of the Bible. Do you own a Bible?

13. What was your image of God or Jesus as a child? How has that image changed over the course of your life?

14. What has happened in your life that has led you to this moment?

15. Describe your background and knowledge of formal religion.

16. What do you think of the way religion is portrayed in movies and on television? Accurate? Not accurate? Not sure?

17. What images of the Catholic Church have you had?

18. Growing up, did you know any Catholics? What was your impression of them?

19. Did you pray as a child? As a teenager? As a young adult? How often? What was it like?

20. What has been your biggest spiritual challenge?

## For Children and Their Families

- When have you felt closest to God?

- Have you heard any stories about God? Tell me one.

- Do you know anyone in your school or neighborhood who believes in God? Tell me about that.

In the first meeting with your inquirer, you want to learn as much as you can about his or her spiritual background. These questions are only suggestions. You do not need to ask all of them. If you can think of other questions that would feel more comfortable to ask, please do. There is no right or wrong. Your only goal in this session is to start to develop a friendship and to learn more about the background of your inquirer.

You should also be sure to leave time for the inquirer to ask questions of you and about the process. It is important to never promise a definite date for initiation or reception (for example, don't say baptism usually happens at the Easter Vigil). Every person's journey is different, and it is impossible to know at this early stage when he or she will be ready.

I think it is important for the inquirer to also learn something of your background and the background of the parish. Try to share some of both during your conversation. You can share some of your own answers to the questions above with your inquirer. When sharing about the background of your parish, here are some possible things to cover.

Talk about the saint or mystery of faith your church is named after. Do you know who founded the parish and why? See if you can find out and share some of that history. Identify your current pastor and how long he has been in the parish. Describe some of the staff members and key committees of the parish. It might help to go over the most recent Sunday bulletin. Point out the different Masses and other prayer events in the parish. If your inquirer is not yet coming to Mass, offer to take him or her to one of the upcoming liturgies.

Keep in mind, however, the most important part of this meeting is to learn about the inquirer. He or she should do most of the talking. I have a 70–30 rule that I use—that is, the inquirers do 70 percent of the talking and 30 percent of the listening. If I am doing most of the talking, inquirers won't "inquire." And I won't learn much about what the inquirers are seeking.

Writing this idea on my computer screen or even talking about it in a workshop makes the concept seem easy enough. In truth, however, not talking is *hard*. When we ask a question, especially one that may seem even a little risky to the seeker, it is very difficult for most of us to just be quiet and *wait for the answer*.

This is where I get tripped up a lot. If I ask a question that is anywhere close to a vulnerable spot in the seekers, their response is going to be silence. They don't yet trust me enough to share their vulnerability. So they have to think about it for a second. They have to decide if they want to answer and then carefully phrase how they are going to answer.

All this usually takes about five seconds. But five seconds is often way too long for me to wait. I tend to jump in and fill the "awkward moment" with a clarification of what I meant or a change of subject. At that point, the other person is off the hook and feels no need to answer me.

One thing that helps is practice. Practice with your spouse or a friend. Ask a question and then wait ten seconds. Then, after you get comfortable with ten seconds of silence, bump it up to twenty. I guarantee you that in your next conversation, if you can insert just three meaningful questions, each followed by at least ten seconds of silence, you will learn way more about your "quiet" inquirer than you ever thought you would.

So remember, the goal is to shift to listening 70 percent of the time and talking no more than 30 percent of the time.

---

If we want to support each other's inner lives, we must remember a simple truth. The human soul does not want to be fixed, it wants simply to be seen and heard. If we want to see and hear a person's soul, there is another truth we must remember. The soul is like a wild animal—tough, resilient, and yet shy. When we go crashing through the woods shouting for it to come out so we can help it, the soul will stay in hiding. But if we are willing to sit quietly and wait for a while, the soul may show itself. (Parker Palmer, *The Courage to Teach*, 156)

In this first meeting, you can use your "Where have you been?" questions to find out about things like previous marriages and any sacraments that might have been celebrated. But don't, at this stage, move into a discussion of annulments or obtaining records. That can come later. Not too much later, but usually not at this first encounter.

In the same vein, if you don't already have it, be sure to get your inquirer's contact information before they leave. However, avoid having your inquirer fill out any kind of form at this meeting. Save that for later so that you can keep this first visit focused on relationship-building. Also, ask how your inquirer best likes to communicate. Many millennials, for example, communicate mostly by text messaging. A lot of baby boomers prefer email.

At the end of your time together, ask the seeker to go home and write down one to three pages about what you discussed about where he or she has been. Ask him or her to bring those pages to your next meeting. Then conclude with a traditional Catholic prayer.

## Active listening

Active listening is different than hearing. An active listener succeeds in hearing not only the words another person is saying but also understanding the meaning of the words *from the speaker's point of view.* Active listening is not a difficult skill to describe, but it is difficult to master. The difficult part is developing the discipline to suspend our own worldview for the five minutes it takes to listen to someone else. There are three steps to active listening:

1. Feedback and verification

2. Clarifying

3. Affirming and validating

*Feedback and verification*

Here's an example of hearing without listening actively:

> Seeker: "I'm not sure God really cares about me."
> Me: "Of course God cares about you. God loves you!"

In my worldview, God loves each of us beyond all imagining. A seeker may not have learned that yet. By correcting the seeker's statement, I'm offering a subtle judgment and not deeply listening to what the seeker is saying. The first key to active listening is feedback and verification. If you aren't used to feeding back what the speaker has told you, it can seem stilted at first. Try it anyway.

> Seeker: "I'm not sure God really cares about me."
> Me: "It sounds like you're not sure about God's care for you.
>     Is that right?"

*Clarifying*

Now, in my worldview, that sounds nuts. How could anyone with eyes and ears not know God's amazing love? But my goal right now is not to assert my point of view. It is to understand what the speaker is trying to communicate. The second key to active listening is asking clarifying questions. We don't have to agree with the speaker. We simply have to get clear enough so we understand why the speaker's statement makes sense to him or her.

> Seeker: "I'm not sure God really cares about me."
> Me: "It sounds like you're not sure about God's care for you.
>     Is that right?"
> Seeker: "Yeah, all the folks in the group talk about how God
>     is so loving, but I don't feel it."
> Me: [confused] "Can you say more about that? I'm not sure
>     I understand what you mean by 'not feeling it.'"

*Affirming and validating*

An active listener needs to ask as many clarifying questions as necessary until the speaker's reasons for his or her beliefs are evident. Once we get why the speaker thinks that way, we need to say so. This is an essential step that often gets lost. The third key to active listening is affirming the speaker's point of view.

> Seeker: "I'm not sure God really cares about me."
> Me: "It sounds like you're not sure about God's care for you. Is that right?"
> Seeker: "Yeah, all the folks in the group talk about how God is so loving, but I don't feel it."
> Me: [confused] "Can you say more about that? I'm not sure I understand what you mean by 'not feeling it.'"
> Seeker: "Well, I lost my job a couple of months ago, and I haven't been able to find a new one. My wife and I are fighting more, and money is really tight. I'm worried we might lose our house if things don't turn around soon. If God cares about me, why doesn't he fix all this?"
> Me: [aha moment] "So if I'm hearing you, you have been out of work a long time. Your financial situation is causing stress in your marriage, and you are worried about losing your home. You think God should fix all this, and he hasn't. Given all that, it totally makes sense why you wonder if God cares about you."

Note that we don't have to *agree* with the speaker's conclusion. We need to ask ourselves, given how the speaker sees things, is the conclusion reasonable? If we understand why he or she came to a given conclusion, we only need to affirm that the conclusion makes sense to the speaker. In this example, helping the seeker learn to see God's love, even in the midst of adversity, is a different agenda and a different skill. The first step is to actively listen to what the person is saying in a way that he or she feels affirmed and validated.

# Chapter 4

## The Second Question

### *Where Are You Now?*

Regarding your habits, knowledge, memories, and attitudes about God, where are you now?

## 20 Different Ways to Ask "Where Are You Now?"

1. Who inspires you? Can you say why?

2. Do you sense a spirit or a higher power in others? Or in the world?

3. Do you love anyone unconditionally? Does anyone love you unconditionally?

4. Where does your happiness come from?

5. How often are you angry or sad?

6. What makes you most anxious?

7. What makes you peaceful?

8. Do you think you have a purpose in life?

9. Do you think there are absolutes in good and evil or right and wrong?

10. What is your image of God?

11. What do you believe about God?

12. How often are you aware of God in your life?

13. What do you know or believe about Jesus?

14. What do you know or believe about Christians?

15. How often do you pray? What is your prayer like?

16. How often do you go to church?

17. Do you ever talk about God with anyone? Describe what that is like.

18. What is your relationship with God like right now? Strong or weak? Like a parent and child? Like a good friend? Distant? Close?

19. What is your family life like?

20. What do you struggle with the most?

## For Children and Their Families

• Tell me a story about who God is and what God does.

• Do you ever talk to God? Does God ever talk to you?

• If you go to church, what is it like? Does it make you happy? Is it fun or boring?

When inquirers come to us, they often ask how they can become Catholic. It is very tempting for us to answer that question. Many times, however, that is not their actual question. If you have been involved in catechumenate ministry for any time at all, you know that most seekers have a deeper issue that has brought them to the point of asking how to become Catholic.

Spiritual author and speaker Ronald Rolheiser, OMI, writes:

> Put more simply, there is within us a fundamental dis-ease, an unquenchable fire that renders us incapable, in this life, of ever coming to full peace. This desire lies at the center of our lives, in the marrow of our bones, and in the deep recesses of the soul. We are not easeful human beings who occasionally get restless, serene persons who once in a while are obsessed by desire. The reverse is true. We are driven persons, forever obsessed, congenitally dis-eased, living lives, as Thoreau once suggested, of quiet desperation, only occasionally experiencing peace. Desire is the straw that stirs the drink. (*The Holy Longing*, 3)

Rolheiser describes this dis-ease:

> Whatever the expression, everyone is ultimately talking about the same thing—an unquenchable fire, a restlessness, a longing, a disquiet, a hunger, a loneliness, a gnawing nostalgia, a wildness that cannot be tamed, a congenital all-embracing ache that lies at the center of human experience and is the ultimate force that drives everything else. This dis-ease is universal. (4)

Often seekers' "dis-ease" has led them to us, and they give a name to their desire as wanting to "become Catholic." Almost always, however, their true desire is deeper and more fundamental.

So when someone asks how to become Catholic, our challenge is to accept the question and also explore more deeply to discover where the question comes from. We are going to do that with our second and third questions: *Where are you now?* and *Where do you want to get to?*

Here are a few things that cause inquirers to explore some big change in their lives, such as becoming Catholic:

- A relationship ends, perhaps due to divorce or death

- A relationship is starting

- Another kind of new beginning (job, city, birth)

- Holiday blues

- Loneliness

- Fear of dying

- Work stress

- Drug or alcohol addiction

- Financial struggles

- Health problems

You can probably name others. What we believe as Catholics is that God embraces us in the very depths of our pain and the heights of our joys. God showers us with mercy and grace. Any and all of the anxieties and fears we have tend to separate us from God. Even a new beginning that makes us happy—a new birth or a new relationship—can also make us anxious. To embrace the new blessing, we have to give up some tried-and-true, comfortable part of ourselves.

These moments of separation are real, and they are often painful. However, they are also moments of grace. Just as physical pain is a warning that something is wrong, spiritual or mental pain is a signal that we need to make a correction in our lives. The realization that change is necessary is a moment of initial conversion. In that moment of seeking change, our role as Christians is to gently introduce the inquirer to the great promise of Jesus—that we will have eternal life and lasting peace, if we turn our hearts to him.

To be able to offer that promise in language that makes sense to the seeker and actually heals his or her wound, we have to discover what the actual need is.

Paulist Father Tony Krisak says that when we are first meeting with seekers, we are not asking them to assent to Catholic doctrine. We are asking them to consider that Jesus is the answer to what they are longing for. And we are telling them that Jesus can heal even their deepest wounds. The way the seeker will discover this truth is to open him- or herself to the action of God's Holy Spirit.

The second question (*Where are you now?*) is designed to encourage the inquirer to explore with you the places in his or her life where the Spirit of God is most active.

If the seeker has no previous Christian formation, he or she may not recognize or acknowledge or be able to name the action of God in his or her life. So some of the questions I've suggested above don't mention God or Jesus. As your friendship with your inquirer grows and a trust relationship develops, you can begin to introduce God into the conversation more. The inquirer obviously has some interest in how God might be a part of his or her life, or else he or she wouldn't be asking about becoming Catholic.

Even so, it is always important to remember that the time of inquiry is a time for the seeker to tell us what is going on in his or her life. It is not a time for us to provide solutions or theological answers. Remember the 70–30 rule: the inquirer talks 70 percent of the time, and you talk 30 percent of the time.

When I meet with inquirers, I tend to group the second and third questions together into one evening meeting that lasts for a total of an hour. So, ideally, I would spend about 20–25 minutes on this second question. However, there are no absolutes in this process of relationship-building. If you need to take more time to explore where your inquirer is right now, by all means do so. Listen closely, and follow where the Spirit leads you.

If in this second meeting, you are not going to continue on with the third question, ask the seeker to go home and write down one to three pages that summarize your discussion of where he or she is now. Ask him or her to bring that summary back to your next meeting. Then conclude with a traditional Catholic prayer.

Let's now turn to the third question.

*Chapter* 5

# The Third Question

## *Where Do You Want to Get To?*

Regarding your habits, knowledge, memories, and attitudes about God, where do you want to get to?

## 20 Different Ways to Ask "Where Do You Want to Get To?"

1. What do you most hope for in your relationship with God?

2. Is there someone (or was there someone) in your life you want to be like in your faith? Describe what it is about that person that makes you want to be like them.

3. Describe what you hope to find in our parish.

4. What attitudes or behaviors do you hope to change in yourself?

5. What are your hopes for your family's faith?

6. What area of knowledge or practice do you want to strengthen with regard to faith?

7. Describe your ideal self one year from now.

8. Describe your ideal relationship with God one year from now.

9. Describe your ideal home life one year from now.

10. What do you hope your prayer life will be like one year from now?

11. What would your life be like if you were to go easier on yourself?

12. What would your life be like if you were a more forgiving person?

13. What would your life be like if you were a more grateful person?

14. What would your life be like if you were a less fearful person?

15. Describe what a perfect day looks like.

16. What do you hope to learn from this process?

17. What are you busy with right now? Will it matter a year from now?

18. What is your most outrageous goal?

19. What is your purpose in life?

20. (If the inquirer answers "I don't know" to any of the above) If you did know, what would the answer be?

## For Children and Their Families

- If you could ask God for a favor, what would you ask?
- Are you ever afraid of anything? What do you think God can do about that?
- When you grow up, who do you most want to be like?

This is a very important question in the formation process. Many inquirers come to us asking what they have to do to become Catholic. It is tempting for RCIA teams to accept that question as the inquirer's goal—to become Catholic. But there is almost always a deeper need, and it is important that we discover that need. If we don't, then shortly after inquirers have accomplished their goal of "becoming Catholic," disappointment is likely to set in. They might have been thinking all along that once they became Catholic, everything would be better. If the process of becoming Catholic doesn't actually meet their deeper needs, the neophytes or new Catholics will very probably drift away from an active involvement in Christian life.

Once we have a clear understanding of the inquirer's present situation (question 2) and a firm grasp on his or her goal (question 3), we will be able to help the inquirer diagnose the gap between those two points. That will lead us to helping the inquirer explore what steps he or she needs to take in order to close the gap (question 4).

The way we ask follow-up questions in this part of the conversation (*Where do you want to get to?*) should help the inquirer discover what competencies or gifts of the Spirit he or she will need to accomplish his or her goal. "Competency" is the ability to do something proficiently. Proficiency is made up of a combination of knowledge, understanding, skill, attitude, and values (see Knowles, *Using Learning Contracts*, 28).

So, for example, if you were a baseball coach developing a learning contract for a rookie player, the rookie might say he or she wanted to get to the point where he or she could hit the ball out of the infield. The rookie might also want to learn how to effectively steal second base. And how to field a ground ball. You can train for those skills and observe how well the rookie is learning. You can also observe his or her attitude toward the disciplines of the game, and you will discover what he or she values about the game. All this will happen by getting the rookie out onto the field to play ball.

In the *Rite of Christian Initiation of Adults*, the church's goal for the seekers is to develop in them "the dispositions that make them fit to take part . . . in the sacraments of initiation" (RCIA 119).

Only those seekers who are "fit" are chosen to take part in the sacraments of initiation (or received into the full communion of the Catholic Church). Fit to do what? God, through the action of the church, chooses those who are able to be disciples of Jesus. Those chosen are expected to be initiated into a life in Christ, which necessarily means a life of mission. Our training process for the seekers is not focused on their knowing enough to assent to Catholic belief. Rather, we train them to take on the rigors of missionary discipleship.

So with seekers, we want to get them "onto the field" as soon as possible, training them in the disciplines of living as Christians. They will learn as we coach them, and we will be able to see what they are learning, what their attitudes are, and what they value.

Some things inquirers have said to me in this conversation include:

- I want to get to the point where I know that God loves me, no matter what.
- I want to no longer be tempted to sin.
- I want to be able to explain God to my daughter.
- I want to stop doubting myself.
- I want to worry less and have less stress in my life.
- I want to have a relationship with God that is strong and unbreakable.
- I want to be more involved with the church.
- I want to learn to pray, and I want to be able to pray every day.
- I want to have faith.
- I want to have peace of mind.
- I want to know more about the Bible.
- I want to not get lost during the Mass.
- I want to stop feeling so negative about myself.

These kinds of desires are at the heart of what various inquirers really mean when they say they want to become Catholic. In academia, we might call these things *learning objectives*. In a faith formation process, we might say these are the call of the Holy Spirit. The Spirit is active in the lives of seekers before we ever meet them. By stirring up these desires in the hearts of people, the Spirit is leading the inquirers to seek God. Some inquirers may not think of what they are doing as "seeking God." However, if they have contacted a Catholic Church and asked about becoming Catholic, they probably have some notion that what they are after is a deeper connection with the divine, a "higher power," or God.

Some of the things that inquirers might say in this conversation could be very broad (for example, "I want to have faith"), and some could be very specific ("I want to be more involved with the church"). During your conversation, you can probe the broad statements for something deeper. And, conversely, you can probe the specific statements for bigger goals the inquirer might be after.

If the inquirer says he or she would like to have more faith, for example, you might ask what having more faith will do for him or her. Why does the inquirer want to have more faith?

If another inquirer is looking to be more involved in the church, you might ask what is going on in the inquirer's life right now that suggests to him or her that being involved in church might be helpful. Is there some bigger reason the inquirer wants to be involved in church?

An important point to notice here is that your inquirers will never state their goals in terms that match the syllabus of a course curriculum. They will never say, for example, they want to know more about things like revelation, the Holy Trinity, the communion of saints, the seven sacraments, morality, and so on. These are objectives the RCIA team might have, but if they are not the objectives of your seekers, providing lectures or videos on subjects like this will have little impact on the faith life of the inquirers.

## The Church's Objectives

In the *Rite of Christian Initiation of Adults*, there are two crucial points of discernment regarding the seeker's journey of faith. The first is the question of faith itself. Has the seeker shown signs of an initial faith that indicate a desire to seek the living God? Most of us have encountered seekers who want to be Catholic but don't really intend to embrace a life of discipleship. In an ideal world, the RCIA asks us to look for these minimum signs of an intent to live as a Christian:

- "evidence of the first faith that was conceived during the period of evangelization"
- evidence of "an initial conversion"
- evidence of an "intention to change their lives"
- evidence of an intention to "enter into a relationship with God in Christ"
- "evidence of the first stirrings of repentance"
- "a start to the practice of calling upon God in prayer"
- "a sense of the Church"
- "some experience of the company and spirit of Christians through contact with a priest or with members of the community" (RCIA 42)

These are the prerequisites for an unbaptized seeker before he or she can celebrate the Rite of Acceptance into the Order of Catechumens. Additionally, we can use these same criteria to discern the willingness of a baptized candidate to take on the rigors of discipleship.

Once an unbaptized person has entered the catechumenate or a baptized person has begun a process for reception into full communion or the celebration of confirmation and Eucharist, the church begins to look for fuller signs of discipleship. These are listed in paragraph 120 (107 in the Canadian rite).

Before celebrating the Rite of Election, the catechumens are expected

> to have undergone a conversion in mind and in action and to have developed a sufficient acquaintance with Christian teaching as well as a spirit of faith and charity. With deliberate will and an enlightened faith, they must have the intention to receive

the sacraments of the Church, a resolve they will express publicly in the actual celebration of the rite.

A baptized candidate will not celebrate the Rite of Election. However, we would expect to see these same signs of discipleship as criteria for their readiness to live as active disciples. Let's look more deeply at each of the three criterion listed in RCIA 120.

## Conversion in Mind and Action

The conversion in mind and action the church is looking for is based on the training process outlined in RCIA 75: "The catechumenate is an extended period during which the candidates are given suitable pastoral formation and guidance, aimed at training them in the Christian life."

The rite then identifies four major areas of training in Christian life for the catechumens: word, community, worship, and witness through apostolic works of mercy.

## A Sufficient Acquaintance with Christian Teaching

The obvious question in this second objective is what is "sufficient"? The answer depends upon several factors. RCIA 5 indicates that "sufficiency" varies for each person, depending upon how the grace of God acts within each one, the individual's level of cooperation with that grace, the action of the church toward each person, and individual circumstances of time and place.

The impact of the many forms of God's grace and of individual circumstances on the readiness of the catechumens for initiation is restated in RCIA 76:

> The duration of the catechumenate will depend on the grace of God and on various circumstances, such as the program of instruction for the catechumenate, the number of catechists, deacons, and priests, the cooperation of the individual catechumens, the means necessary for them to come to the site of the catechumenate and spend time there, the help of the local community.

RCIA 76 also says that because of the highly individualized nature of what can be considered sufficient preparation, there can be no standard measure for knowing how long it will take for a person to be ready: "Nothing, therefore, can be settled a priori."

The key criterion to determine sufficiency is, can this catechumen now live the Christian life? Does he or she not only have "an appropriate acquaintance with dogmas and precepts," but does he or she also have "a profound sense of the mystery of salvation" (75.1)?

## Spirit of Faith and Charity

An important factor in the initiation of seekers is that they develop a "spirit of faith and charity." This is not only an intellectual faith and a kind feeling toward others. This is a heartfelt faith that leads to active service of others. It is a faith that will be made visible in the actions of the seekers. RCIA 75.4 says that this spirit of faith and charity is not merely an internal feeling. It is an active work, along with others, to spread the Gospel. The catechumens' spirit of faith and charity is manifest in "the witness of their lives" and the proclamation of their faith.

## The Bishop's Concerns

Another place you will find the church's objectives is in the Rite of Election. At RCIA 131[B], the "Affirmation by the Godparents," the bishop asks three questions of the godparents about their catechumens:

- "Have they faithfully listened to God's word proclaimed by the Church?"

- "Have they responded to that word and begun to walk in God's presence?"

- "Have they shared the company of their Christian brothers and sisters and joined with them in prayer?"

The parallels to the requirements found in RCIA 120 and RCIA 75 are obvious. The first question echoes the emphasis on the catechumens having "developed a sufficient acquaintance with Christian teaching," which is derived from the living word of God.

The second question about walking in God's presence is a metaphorical one. What does it mean to walk in God's presence? At this point, it should be obvious to the catechumens and their godparents that to walk in God's presence is to exhibit a "spirit of faith and charity." The bishop's second question also resonates with the requirement that the catechumens "have undergone a conversion in mind and in action."

The third question is more clearly linked to RCIA 75.2 and 75.3, which focus on the need to apprentice catechumens in the life of the Christian community and a life of prayer and worship.

## Aligning Objectives

Just as we know the inquirers are not going to self-identify objectives such as knowing more about things like revelation, the Holy Trinity, the communion of saints, etc., neither will they list these three exact requirements from RCIA 120. However, if you look at some of the examples I listed above of actual objectives seekers have identified for themselves, many of them sound very much like the kinds of objectives listed in RCIA 120.

On occasion, we will encounter inquirers whose objectives are not clearly aligned with the objectives of the church. Those inquirers are often not really seeking a relationship with God. For example, they want to marry a Catholic and someone told them they have to become Catholic themselves first. Or, in some countries, they want to teach in Catholic schools, and the schools only hire Catholics. Or they want to enroll their children in Catholic schools at a discounted tuition rate.

If you encounter people who are not really seeking a relationship with God, think of them as folks who need to hear the Good News. Perhaps through your conversations with them, they will open up to a desire for something deeper. In any case, as long as they are only using the initiation process as a means to an end, the RCIA team and the pastor will have to decide the best course of action. You could possibly delay their initiation until you see some signs of faith, such as those listed in RCIA 42. Or you could let them proceed, knowing that their hearts are not in it, and pray for their eventual conversion. It is a difficult situation that doesn't have a black-and-white solution.

In my experience, however, the vast majority of seekers do have some level of at least initial faith and a true desire for a deep, intimate relationship with God. Our next question, then, will start to lay the foundation for a faith formation plan.

If you combined questions 2 and 3 into one session, at the end of your conversation, ask the seeker to return to your next meeting with a one- to three-page summary of "Where are you now?" and another one to three pages on "Where do you want to get to?" Then conclude with a traditional Catholic prayer.

Chapter 6

# The Fourth Question

## *How Are You Going to Get to Where You Want to Go?*

Regarding your habits, knowledge, memories, and attitudes about God, how are you going to get to where you want to go?

### 20 Different Ways to Ask "How Are You Going to Get to Where You Want to Go?"

1. In what ways do you need to develop your faith practices to get where you want to go?

2. In what ways do you need to develop your relationship with God?

3. In what ways do you need to develop your relationship with the church?

4. How do you need your family to support you?

5. How do you need the faith community at this parish to support you?

6. How will you determine if your plan will get you where you want to go?

7. How will you monitor your progress toward your goal?

8. How will you get feedback on your progress?

9. What is your tentative timeline for getting to where you want to go?

10. How will you identify and develop the skills you need to get to where you want to go?

11. What are some resources you think you might need along the way?

12. What kind of activities, conversations, reading, or mentoring would be helpful?

13. What kind of regular reflection or writing process would be helpful?

14. What level of priority will this process have in your life?

15. What skills do you already have that will help you in this process? What skills do you need to develop?

16. What obstacles do you have to overcome to get to where you want to go?

17. What are the next three steps you have to take to get started on this process?

18. How will you sustain yourself if the process becomes difficult or frustrating?

19. How will you identify markers of success and progress along the way?

20. What do you have to let go of in order to get where you want to go?

## For Children and Their Families

- If you wanted to get to know God better, what would you do?

- What might get in the way of you getting to know God better?

- How can your mom and dad (or grandparents) help you get to know God better?

This fourth question is, perhaps, the one that highlights the greatest difference between how children learn and how adults learn. Generally, adults tend to have a more problem-centered or task-centered focus on their learning needs. Children tend to be more subject-centered. Contract learning gives adults the opportunity to identify their own objectives and then create a plan for reaching those objectives. (See Knowles, *Using Learning Contracts*, 42.)

The previous question (*Where do you want to get to?*) helped the inquirer identify the gap between the present situation and the ideal situation with regard to his or her habits, knowledge, memories, and attitudes about God. Both you and the inquirer now know the hoped-for outcome of the initiation process.

This next step creates a plan for closing the gap. And creating that plan is primarily the job of the inquirer.

To make the inquirer primarily responsible for the plan is a dramatic shift in what many of us believe our role as catechists to be. Knowles says this about the roles of instructors and learners:

> In essence, in contract learning the role of the instructor shifts from that of a didactic transmitter of content and controller of leaners to that of a facilitator of self-directed learning and content resource (or broker). (*Using Learning Contracts*, 43)

To make this transition, Knowles says that he had to make three critical adjustments. He had to:

1. shift from "instructor" to "counselor" or "consultant";

2. identify what new skills he would need to develop in this new role;

3. experience a greater psychic reward that comes from "releasing rather than controlling the energy of learners" (*Using Learning Contracts*, 43–44).

When I first tried adapting the contract learning process to faith formation, I have to admit there was an adjustment process. When I was new to catechumenate ministry, I was very "teacherly." I got better over the years, and I like to think I had already become less of an instructor and more of a guide. But the shift to a contract learning process was a new level for me. I had to shift from being a "catechist" to being a "mentor."

I knew how to be a mentor in other areas of my life, so I worked to bring those skills over into the catechumenate process. Writing about it here, the shift from catechist to mentor seems easy to conceive of. But in practice, it took some effort on my part. As a catechist, I had gotten very good at breaking down complex ideas into simple concepts, and I could deliver those concepts in an engaging way.

I had to let go of that skill and replace it with the skills I'd need to be an effective mentor. Next, I had to identify and strengthen the skills I'd need to be an effective mentor. Specifically, I had to let the seekers take more of a lead. I had to let them try things and make mistakes. I had to know when to challenge them and when to be patient.

And most of all, I had to find a new benefit for *me* in the process. Before, I had gotten a high level of satisfaction from being able to explain the core teachings of the church in clear, accessible language. While that satisfaction benefits me, it's not necessarily a benefit to the seekers. So the personal benefit I strive for now is to revel in the joy I experience when I see how involved inquirers become when they take charge of their own learning.

That shift in identifying my personal benefit was relatively easy for me, but it can be difficult for career teachers or catechists who have so far found their joy in traditional lecture-style teaching.

Another worry that some catechists have is that if the seekers take charge of their own learning, they won't yet know enough to be able to develop a comprehensive plan for training in Christian life.

The key is to remember that the creation of a faith formation plan is a negotiation between companions—you and the seekers. If we keep in mind that the inquirers are *already* following the promptings of the Holy Spirit, we can more easily envision ourselves as mentors who guide them in the best way to respond to those promptings. If, at first, the inquirers propose learning activities that fall short of what we know they will need to prepare for the next phase of their journey, then we should absolutely assist them in rounding out their plan. The shift we need to make, however, is to move out of the role of a "teacher" setting a curriculum and into the role of a "coach" assisting talented protégés in maximizing their gifts.

Perhaps the most common objection I encounter when we start thinking about each inquirer developing his or her own faith formation plan is that there isn't enough time. With our already-packed schedules, how can we make time to coach each inquirer individually through this process?

The fact is, you will probably spend less time in a contract learning process than you will if you use a didactic lecture-style process. Malcolm Knowles, whose contract learning process is significantly more involved than the simplified version I am proposing, wrote:

> I find that I can serve as many students as a contract learning mentor as I did as a didactic teacher; I simply use my time and energy differently. (*Using Learning Contracts*, 45)

For me, the most exciting and rewarding part of the contract learning process applied to faith formation happens when we delve into the final question. We will cover that in the next chapter.

Don't forget, if you are not going to continue on with the fifth question in this session, ask the seeker to go home and write down one to three pages that summarize your discussion of "How are you going to get to where you want to go?" Ask him or her to bring that summary back to your next meeting. Then conclude with a traditional Catholic prayer.

## Setting goals for ourselves

If we are going to help seekers set their goals, we have to also set goals for ourselves. Many of us tend to think of practical goals—goals that make sense and that are actually doable. I think, though, if we are going to be forming seekers to live as disciples of Jesus, we have to shake off this self-limiting attitude.

If you think about it, it's actually a form of idolatry. Idolatry is worship of an image or idea that is not God. When we adore the practical, we are turning our face away from the unlimited possibility of the Divine. Nelson Mandela is the personification of someone who refused to settle for the practical. In his inauguration speech (quoting Marianne Williamson), he said, "Your playing small does not serve the world. Who are you not to be great?"

So what would make you great? What is it you really want? What is your biggest limit? What is holding you back from everything God is calling you to be? If someone gave you unlimited resources (money, time, people, space), what is it you would do? Write that down, and believe that the Holy Spirit has given you the gifts you need to reach your highest goal.

# Chapter 7

# The Fifth Question

## *How Will You Know You Have Arrived?*

Regarding your habits, knowledge, memories, and attitudes about God, how will you know you have arrived?

### 20 Different Ways to Ask "How Will You Know You Have Arrived?"

1. How will you know if you've met your goal?

2. How will your family know?

3. How will others you interact with know?

4. How will the people at this parish know?

5. What changes will you see in your prayer life?

6. What changes will you see in your family life?

7. What changes will you see in how you spend your time?

8. How will your values have changed?

9. How will you know if you have become more forgiving?

10. How will you know if you have become more flexible?

11. How will you know if you have become more generous?

12. How will you know if you have become more hopeful?

13. How will you know if you have become more joyful?

14. How will strangers recognize that you are living a Christian life?

15. What regular practices or habits will you have implemented?

16. What new knowledge will you have acquired?

17. What new skills will you have learned?

18. What new beliefs will you have gained?

19. What will you no longer be worried about?

20. How will you handle setbacks?

## For Children and Their Families

- How do you think the kids in school or in your neighborhood would act around you if you and God were good friends?

- Do you think you would act any differently if you knew God was with you all the time?

- How would you be different around your parents or brothers and sisters?

This final question is the most exciting for me because it changes the dynamic of who is ultimately responsible for discerning the readiness of the inquirer to move forward along the process. In other words, I never have to answer the inquirer's question, "When can I be baptized?" In the development of the faith formation plan, the inquirers set out the criteria for readiness and they hold themselves accountable for being ready.

Remember, however, that as a mentor and coach, you are not completely passive in this process. The church has criteria for readiness for the various stages in the initiation process. Your role will be to negotiate with the inquirers to ensure that their markers for readiness align with those of the church.

When we are talking about unbaptized inquirers, the *Rite of Christian Initiation of Adults* lists several criteria that must be in place before they can celebrate the Rite of Acceptance into the Order of Catechumens:

- "the beginnings of the spiritual life"

- "the fundamentals of Christian teaching have taken root"

- "evidence of the first faith"

- evidence of "an initial conversion"

- "intention to change their lives"

- "evidence of the first stirrings of repentance"

- "a start to the practice of calling upon God in prayer"

- "a sense of the Church"

- "some experience of the company and spirit of Christians" (RCIA 42)

If you look at those criteria closely, they make up a very low bar. They are conditioned by words such as *beginnings, initial, first, some, start,* and *intention.* The inquirers do not always have to demonstrate each of these qualities consistently. Mostly, they have to *want to* live this way. Many inquirers come us to already possessing these desires. So their preparation time for the Rite of Acceptance can be very short.

The bar for celebrating the Rite of Election is higher. In this case, the catechumens will have to show that they are capable of living as Christians. Specifically, the church is looking for:

- "a conversion in mind and in action"

- "a sufficient acquaintance with Christian teaching"

- "a spirit of faith and charity"
- "the intention to receive the sacraments of the Church"
- "a resolve [to express their intention] publicly in the actual celebration of the rite" (RCIA 120; 107 in the Canadian rite)

If your inquirers are baptized, they will have had varying levels of formation and will be more or less proficient at living a Christian life. If they have little or no formation, you can help them form their criteria for readiness listed in RCIA 42 in ways that are similar to the unbaptized inquirers. If they have already been formed to live as Christians, you can look for the criteria listed in RCIA 120. If, through their responses to the first two questions, they are already showing that they know how to live a Christian life, their preparation for either the completion of their initiation or reception into full communion can be very short.

If it seems helpful, you can also provide your seekers with the "Goal-Setting Worksheet for Becoming a Disciple" provided in appendix 2. They can assess their own progress toward their goals throughout their formation process.

If you combined questions 4 and 5 into one session, ask the seeker to return to your next meeting with a one- to three-page summary of "How are you going to get to where you want to go?" and another one to three pages on "How will you know you have arrived?" Then conclude with a traditional Catholic prayer.

# Chapter 8

# Creating a Faith Formation Plan

As I have mentioned, after each meeting with an inquirer, I ask him or her to write one to three pages on what we talked about and bring those pages back to me at the next session. If you cover more than one of the five major questions in a session, the inquirer would write one to three pages on each question. If you think it would be helpful, you can give the inquirer a copy of the major question and several of the different ways you asked the question to help him or her remember what you talked about.

When I do this process, once I have all the pages back from an inquirer, I'll spend some time alone in prayer asking the Holy Spirit to guide both me and the inquirer as I prepare an initial faith formation plan.

To create the plan, I work in a spreadsheet with two columns. You can also create the plan on a blank sheet of paper, divided into two columns. The left column is what the inquirer expects to accomplish, learn, or do. The right column is what the church expects the inquirer to accomplish, learn, or do.

It looks like this:

# Jane Smith's Formation Plan
## St. Mildgytha Parish
### [DATE]

| | Jane's expectations | The church's expectations |
|---|---|---|
| **Goals**<br><br>(Derived from the seeker's replies to the questions, especially "Where do I want to get to?") | | |
| **Plan**<br><br>(Derived from the seeker's replies to the questions, especially "How will I get to where I want to go?") | | |
| **Evaluation**<br><br>(Derived from the seeker's replies to the questions, especially "How will I know I have arrived?") | | |

The left column would include anything the inquirer wrote about or said to you. Try to stick as closely as possible to the inquirer's actual words. The right column would be a restatement of the inquirer's words, using the language of the church. It would also include any necessary requirements that the inquirer may have left out.

What kinds of things have to be included in the faith formation plan? Remember what we said in chapter 5 about the church's objectives, listed in RCIA 120 (Canadian rite, 107):

Before the Rite of Election is celebrated, the catechumens are expected

- "to have undergone a conversion in mind and in action"

- "and to have developed a sufficient acquaintance with Christian teaching"

- "as well as a spirit of faith and charity."

- "With deliberate will and an enlightened faith they must have the intention to receive the sacraments of the Church, a resolve they will express publicly in the actual celebration of the rite."

Review what we said in chapter 5 about aligning the objectives of the inquirer with the church's objectives as you begin to write the faith formation plan. See the example below.

Once you think the plan represents what the inquirer said, schedule a meeting to go over it with him or her. Ask the seeker if the plan, as you have summarized it, reflects what the two of you discussed. Ask the seeker if he or she thinks the plan is feasible. Make any adjustments that might be necessary, and then pray with the seeker as he or she begins this new journey. If you like, you can adapt one of the prayers from Blessing of the Catechumens in the *Rite of Christian Initiation of Adults* (see paragraph 97).

# Jane Smith's Formation Plan
## St. Mildgytha Parish
## [DATE]

| | Jane's expectations | The church's expectations |
|---|---|---|
| **Goals** | With God's help, become a better person | Understand the church's teaching on right behavior |
| | Become more patient with my daughters | Do daily examination of conscience |
| | As a family, become more involved in church | Regularly participate in parish activities |
| | Learn more about the Bible | Weekly reflection on the readings for Sunday |
| | Learn the prayers of the church | Develop a daily prayer practice, including examination of conscience |
| | Not get lost during the Mass | Participate in Mass every Sunday; participate in catechetical sessions |
| | Strengthen my relationship with God | Understand the mission of Jesus; look for daily "God sightings" |

| | | |
|---|---|---|
| **Plan** | Develop a prayer routine | Develop a daily prayer practice, including examination of conscience |
| | Schedule time to be involved in the parish | Regularly participate in parish activities |
| | Get parents and friends to come to Mass with me | Develop a practice of evangelization |
| | Continue coming to Mass every Sunday | Participate in Mass every Sunday |
| | Continue praying | Practice daily prayer |

| | | |
|---|---|---|
| **Evaluation** | I will feel God more in my heart My family and friends will see a different Jane St. Mildgytha parishioners will see more of me | |

# A New Way of Thinking about Formation

It is important to think about the faith formation plan as being the *inquirer's* plan. It is not your plan for the inquirer. Knowles has his students write their own plans and bring them to him for review. I opted instead to write each plan myself (or have another team member write it), but using the exact words of the inquirer. My intuition tells me that writing the plan myself may provide a more comprehensive and more fruitful plan for the inquirer. Even so, I bring the plan back to the inquirer and ask him or her if it represents what was said and what the inquirer actually wants to do. I emphasize that it is his or her plan, not mine. The inquirer has to own it and be responsible for it. If he or she wants to make any amendments to the plan, we make them.

# What If the Plan Is Missing Something?

Whenever I describe this process to RCIA teams, they worry that the inquirer will make a plan that leaves out crucial elements. I have never found that to be true. I am consistently amazed at the depth of responses that come from this simple process. Inquirers often require far more of themselves than I would ask of them.

If you do happen to encounter an inquirer who is missing something essential from the plan—weekly participation in Sunday liturgy, for example—you can add it in as part of the church's expectations. It is crucial, however, that as RCIA team members, we begin to think of the faith formation process very differently than we may be used to. For lasting, lifelong formation to begin to sprout, we have to make that crucial shift from being instructors to being mentors.

You will, however, sometimes encounter inquirers who are not really seeking a relationship with God. When that has happened to me, we never got as far as making a plan. They did not return their written reflections, or they did not show up for one or more of the meetings at which we would go over the five questions. I switch my thinking when this happens. I'm no longer trying to help a seeker begin a process of lifelong formation. Instead, I need to be evangelizing. I try to keep in touch with the seeker. I try to maintain a relationship. And I emphasize that I'm always available any time the seeker wants to reconnect or continue the conversation.

Once the inquirers have plans that they believe are truly their own and are ready to take responsibility for them, our next step is to help them implement those plans. That's what we will look at next.

*Chapter* 9

# Implementing the Plan

The *Rite of Christian Initiation of Adults* never mentions an "RCIA team." That is because the church does not regard the initiation of catechumens to be a specialized ministry. Initiation, in the way the RCIA envisions it, is part of the normal activities of being a parishioner and the daily practice of living as a baptized person. Specifically, the church teaches:

> The people of God, as represented by the local Church, should understand and show by their concern that *the initiation of adults is the responsibility of all the baptized.* Therefore the community must always be fully prepared in the pursuit of its apostolic vocation to give help to those who are searching for Christ. (9, emphasis added)

Usually, when RCIA teams read that paragraph, they throw up their hands in frustration. They start to list all the times they tried and failed to get parishioners more involved in the process. What most teams have tried to do, however, is to get parishioners to act in ways that are not part of their "apostolic vocation."

Our apostolic vocation is the way we live out our baptism and our call to holiness. St. Paul tells us that, together, we all make up the Body of Christ. But each of us has a specific role within the Body (see 1 Cor 12:27). Just as an eye cannot fulfill the role of the ear, so too, a Communion minister cannot fulfill the role of a catechist. When you want to involve the larger parish in the initiation process, instead of bringing parishioners into your RCIA session to *talk about* their ministries, take the seekers out into the parish to *show* them how people serve. Showing is much more effective than talking.

What the RCIA means by having the community initiate through its apostolic vocation is that we take the catechumens out into the community, where "apostolicity" is happening. The catechumens then learn what it is to live like apostles when they see members of the community do so in the real world.

There are four ways in which the Christian community pursues its apostolic vocation:

1. We live in ways that are faithful to God's word and the teaching of the apostles (see RCIA 75.1).

2. We live together in a community of love, striving, with God's grace, to be ethical, moral, forgiving, and holy (see RCIA 75.2).

3. We rejoice that God has acted in our lives, especially through the life, death, and resurrection of Jesus; we express our joy through constant prayer and worship, especially in the Sunday Eucharist (see RCIA 75.3).

4. Our joy overflows into the world where we are compelled to share the good news of God's unconditional love with every person (see RCIA 75.4).

## Centrality of Sunday

The core of this formation process for every seeker will be participation in the community's worship on the Lord's Day. The centrality of worship on the Lord's Day should become obvious to the seeker during the evangelization period. If it has not become obvious, evangelization has not yet resulted in the minimum requirements for celebrating the Rite of Acceptance.

Sometimes the centrality of worship on the Lord's Day is not obvious to the RCIA team. I've encountered teams who insist that the seekers be present for a minimum number of formation sessions, but they are somewhat less insistent about participation in Sunday worship. "We told them Sunday Mass is obligatory, but they just don't come" is the complaint RCIA teams often lodge. Sometimes these RCIA teams will still send catechumens who have not been participating in Sunday worship to the Rite of Election for fear of "holding back" someone from the rest of the "class."

We have to let go of the notion that training in an apostolic life is accomplished in a classroom. One learns to live apostolically by doing what the apostolic community does. If one is *not* doing what the community does, that person needs to remain in the training process—the catechumenate—until there is evidence of joining in the pursuit of the community's apostolic vocation. In other words, you will know it's time to make a catechumen a Christian when you see him or her living as a Christian.

For someone who has had little or no previous exposure to Christianity, the training process will take at least one full liturgical year. In fact, the RCIA says it could take "several years if necessary" (RCIA 76). The training process must take at least one full liturgical year because it is in the celebration of the liturgical year that the church "unfolds the whole mystery of Christ" (Constitution on the Sacred Liturgy, 102). We cannot say that someone who has never encountered the mystery of Christ can possibly be ready to live as a Christian until—at the very least—he or she has been formed in the whole of that mystery.

The core of a good formation plan has to include the four key training areas identified in RCIA 75. The seekers need to learn how to live a life in Christ that is solidly rooted in the **word** of God, incorporated into the Christian **community**, marked by prayer and **worship**, and dedicated to **witness and service**. If a seeker is participating in Mass every Sunday, he or she is being formed in each of these areas of Christian life. So Sunday worship must be the foundation of any formation process. Many of our baptized candidates are already living out some or all of these areas of Christian life. For them, their formation periods may not take as much time as those of uncatechized seekers. However, for seekers who have had little or no previous experience of living as a Christian, they will need to spend at least one full liturgical year in formation.

## Year-Round Process

Imagining a year-round catechumenate is a roadblock for many teams. They just don't believe it is practical for them to keep an RCIA process going all year long. What stops them is that they imagine doubling or tripling the amount of work they are currently doing in order to cover all the weeks of the year. And providing weekly catechetical sessions for fifty-two weeks of the year seems overwhelming. As a result, they continue to use a school-year model.

But let's imagine your Rite of Acceptance is scheduled for the first Sunday in October and you plan to meet weekly with the catechumens after that. So that's four sessions in October. There are another four Sundays in November, but you probably aren't meeting Thanksgiving week. Nor Christmas week in December nor New Year's Week in January. For this example, let's say Ash Wednesday falls on February 10. That means, between October and Ash Wednesday, you might have fourteen catechetical sessions with the catechumens.

When I suggest a year-round catechumenate, I am not suggesting you add any more catechetical sessions beyond what your team is currently offering. If you are offering fourteen sessions, for example, you have the option of continuing to offer those same sessions. However, we are going to spread out the sessions over all the seasons of the liturgical year.

If you changed your school-year schedule—from meeting once a week, October to Easter—to meeting once a month, from October of one year, through the end of the following year, and up to the next Ash Wednesday, *you would be meeting seventeen times* over a more relaxed schedule. You can even "take summer off," skipping the July and August meetings and still retain the same number of catechetical sessions as in a school-year model.

# Cycling through the Liturgical Year

Just because you are not meeting for weekly sessions does not mean you will not be interacting with the catechumens. *They will still be participating in the Liturgy of the Word every Sunday* with their sponsors and the rest of the parish.

*Figure 1: A school-year calendar showing fourteen meeting days.*
*October through Ash Wednesday*

## Catechetical Calendar — School-Year Model

| October | | | | | | |
| Su | M | Tu | W | Th | F | Sa |
| --- | --- | --- | --- | --- | --- | --- |
|  |  |  |  | 1 | 2 | 3 |
| 4 | 5 | 6 | 7 | 8 | 9 | 10 |
| 11 | 12 | 13 | 14 | 15 | 16 | 17 |
| 18 | 19 | 20 | 21 | 22 | 23 | 24 |
| 25 | 26 | 27 | 28 | 29 | 30 | 31 |

| November | | | | | | |
| Su | M | Tu | W | Th | F | Sa |
| --- | --- | --- | --- | --- | --- | --- |
| 1 | 2 | 3 | 4 | 5 | 6 | 7 |
| 8 | 9 | 10 | 11 | 12 | 13 | 14 |
| 15 | 16 | 17 | 18 | 19 | 20 | 21 |
| 22 | 23 | 24 | 25 | 26 | 27 | 28 |
| 29 | 30 |  |  |  |  |  |

| December | | | | | | |
| Su | M | Tu | W | Th | F | Sa |
| --- | --- | --- | --- | --- | --- | --- |
|  |  | 1 | 2 | 3 | 4 | 5 |
| 6 | 7 | 8 | 9 | 10 | 11 | 12 |
| 13 | 14 | 15 | 16 | 17 | 18 | 19 |
| 20 | 21 | 22 | 23 | 24 | 25 | 26 |
| 27 | 28 | 29 | 30 | 31 |  |  |

| January | | | | | | |
| Su | M | Tu | W | Th | F | Sa |
| --- | --- | --- | --- | --- | --- | --- |
|  |  |  |  |  | 1 | 2 |
| 3 | 4 | 5 | 6 | 7 | 8 | 9 |
| 10 | 11 | 12 | 13 | 14 | 15 | 16 |
| 17 | 18 | 19 | 20 | 21 | 22 | 23 |
| 24 | 25 | 26 | 27 | 28 | 29 | 30 |
| 31 |  |  |  |  |  |  |

| February | | | | | | |
| Su | M | Tu | W | Th | F | Sa |
| --- | --- | --- | --- | --- | --- | --- |
|  | 1 | 2 | 3 | 4 | 5 | 6 |
| 7 | 8 | 9 | 10 | 11 | 12 | 13 |
| 14 | 15 | 16 | 17 | 18 | 19 | 20 |
| 21 | 22 | 23 | 24 | 25 | 26 | 27 |
| 28 | 29 |  |  |  |  |  |

| March | | | | | | |
| Su | M | Tu | W | Th | F | Sa |
| --- | --- | --- | --- | --- | --- | --- |
|  |  | 1 | 2 | 3 | 4 | 5 |
| 6 | 7 | 8 | 9 | 10 | 11 | 12 |
| 13 | 14 | 15 | 16 | 17 | 18 | 19 |
| 20 | 21 | 22 | 23 | 24 | 25 | 26 |
| 27 | 28 | 29 | 30 | 31 |  |  |

*Figure 2: A year-round calendar showing seventeen meeting days.*

## Catechetical Calendar — Year-Round Model

| October | | | | | | |
| Su | M | Tu | W | Th | F | Sa |
| --- | --- | --- | --- | --- | --- | --- |
|  |  |  |  | 1 | 2 | 3 |
| 4 | 5 | 6 | 7 | 8 | 9 | 10 |
| 11 | 12 | 13 | 14 | 15 | 16 | 17 |
| 18 | 19 | 20 | 21 | 22 | 23 | 24 |
| 25 | 26 | 27 | 28 | 29 | 30 | 31 |

| November | | | | | | |
| Su | M | Tu | W | Th | F | Sa |
| --- | --- | --- | --- | --- | --- | --- |
| 1 | 2 | 3 | 4 | 5 | 6 | 7 |
| 8 | 9 | 10 | 11 | 12 | 13 | 14 |
| 15 | 16 | 17 | 18 | 19 | 20 | 21 |
| 22 | 23 | 24 | 25 | 26 | 27 | 28 |
| 29 | 30 |  |  |  |  |  |

| December | | | | | | |
| Su | M | Tu | W | Th | F | Sa |
| --- | --- | --- | --- | --- | --- | --- |
|  |  | 1 | 2 | 3 | 4 | 5 |
| 6 | 7 | 8 | 9 | 10 | 11 | 12 |
| 13 | 14 | 15 | 16 | 17 | 18 | 19 |
| 20 | 21 | 22 | 23 | 24 | 25 | 26 |
| 27 | 28 | 29 | 30 | 31 |  |  |

| January | | | | | | |
|---|---|---|---|---|---|---|
| Su | M | Tu | W | Th | F | Sa |
| | | | | | 1 | 2 |
| 3 | 4 | 5 | 6 | 7 | 8 | 9 |
| 10 | 11 | 12 | 13 | 14 | 15 | 16 |
| 17 | 18 | 19 | 20 | 21 | 22 | 23 |
| 24 | 25 | 26 | 27 | 28 | 29 | 30 |
| 31 | | | | | | |

| February | | | | | | |
|---|---|---|---|---|---|---|
| Su | M | Tu | W | Th | F | Sa |
| | 1 | 2 | 3 | 4 | 5 | 6 |
| 7 | 8 | 9 | 10 | 11 | 12 | 13 |
| 14 | 15 | 16 | 17 | 18 | 19 | 20 |
| 21 | 22 | 23 | 24 | 25 | 26 | 27 |
| 28 | 29 | | | | | |

| March | | | | | | |
|---|---|---|---|---|---|---|
| Su | M | Tu | W | Th | F | Sa |
| | | 1 | 2 | 3 | 4 | 5 |
| 6 | 7 | 8 | 9 | 10 | 11 | 12 |
| 13 | 14 | 15 | 16 | 17 | 18 | 19 |
| 20 | 21 | 22 | 23 | 24 | 25 | 26 |
| 27 | 28 | 29 | 30 | 31 | | |

| April | | | | | | |
|---|---|---|---|---|---|---|
| Su | M | Tu | W | Th | F | Sa |
| | | | | | 1 | 2 |
| 3 | 4 | 5 | 6 | 7 | 8 | 9 |
| 10 | 11 | 12 | 13 | 14 | 15 | 16 |
| 17 | 18 | 19 | 20 | 21 | 22 | 23 |
| 24 | 25 | 26 | 27 | 28 | 29 | 30 |

| May | | | | | | |
|---|---|---|---|---|---|---|
| Su | M | Tu | W | Th | F | Sa |
| 1 | 2 | 3 | 4 | 5 | 6 | 7 |
| 8 | 9 | 10 | 11 | 12 | 13 | 14 |
| 15 | 16 | 17 | 18 | 19 | 20 | 21 |
| 22 | 23 | 24 | 25 | 26 | 27 | 28 |
| 29 | 30 | 31 | | | | |

| June | | | | | | |
|---|---|---|---|---|---|---|
| Su | M | Tu | W | Th | F | Sa |
| | | | 1 | 2 | 3 | 4 |
| 5 | 6 | 7 | 8 | 9 | 10 | 11 |
| 12 | 13 | 14 | 15 | 16 | 17 | 18 |
| 19 | 20 | 21 | 22 | 23 | 24 | 25 |
| 26 | 27 | 28 | 29 | 30 | | |

| July | | | | | | |
|---|---|---|---|---|---|---|
| Su | M | Tu | W | Th | F | Sa |
| | | | | | 1 | 2 |
| 3 | 4 | 5 | 6 | 7 | 8 | 9 |
| 10 | 11 | 12 | 13 | 14 | 15 | 16 |
| 17 | 18 | 19 | 20 | 21 | 22 | 23 |
| 24 | 25 | 26 | 27 | 28 | 29 | 30 |
| 31 | | | | | | |

| August | | | | | | |
|---|---|---|---|---|---|---|
| Su | M | Tu | W | Th | F | Sa |
| | 1 | 2 | 3 | 4 | 5 | 6 |
| 7 | 8 | 9 | 10 | 11 | 12 | 13 |
| 14 | 15 | 16 | 17 | 18 | 19 | 20 |
| 21 | 22 | 23 | 24 | 25 | 26 | 27 |
| 28 | 29 | 30 | 31 | | | |

| September | | | | | | |
|---|---|---|---|---|---|---|
| Su | M | Tu | W | Th | F | Sa |
| | | | | 1 | 2 | 3 |
| 4 | 5 | 6 | 7 | 8 | 9 | 10 |
| 11 | 12 | 13 | 14 | 15 | 16 | 17 |
| 18 | 19 | 20 | 21 | 22 | 23 | 24 |
| 25 | 26 | 27 | 28 | 29 | 30 | |

| October | | | | | | |
|---|---|---|---|---|---|---|
| Su | M | Tu | W | Th | F | Sa |
| | | | | | | 1 |
| 2 | 3 | 4 | 5 | 6 | 7 | 8 |
| 9 | 10 | 11 | 12 | 13 | 14 | 15 |
| 16 | 17 | 18 | 19 | 20 | 21 | 22 |
| 23 | 24 | 25 | 26 | 27 | 28 | 29 |
| 30 | 31 | | | | | |

| November | | | | | | |
|---|---|---|---|---|---|---|
| Su | M | Tu | W | Th | F | Sa |
| | | 1 | 2 | 3 | 4 | 5 |
| 6 | 7 | 8 | 9 | 10 | 11 | 12 |
| 13 | 14 | 15 | 16 | 17 | 18 | 19 |
| 20 | 21 | 22 | 23 | 24 | 25 | 26 |
| 27 | 28 | 29 | 30 | | | |

| December | | | | | | |
|---|---|---|---|---|---|---|
| Su | M | Tu | W | Th | F | Sa |
| | | | | 1 | 2 | 3 |
| 4 | 5 | 6 | 7 | 8 | 9 | 10 |
| 11 | 12 | 13 | 14 | 15 | 16 | 17 |
| 18 | 19 | 20 | 21 | 22 | 23 | 24 |
| 25 | 26 | 27 | 28 | 29 | 30 | 31 |

| January | | | | | | |
|---|---|---|---|---|---|---|
| Su | M | Tu | W | Th | F | Sa |
| 1 | 2 | 3 | 4 | 5 | 6 | 7 |
| 8 | 9 | 10 | 11 | 12 | 13 | 14 |
| 15 | 16 | 17 | 18 | 19 | 20 | 21 |
| 22 | 23 | 24 | 25 | 26 | 27 | 28 |
| 29 | 30 | 31 | | | | |

| February | | | | | | |
|---|---|---|---|---|---|---|
| Su | M | Tu | W | Th | F | Sa |
| | | | 1 | 2 | 3 | 4 |
| 5 | 6 | 7 | 8 | 9 | 10 | 11 |
| 12 | 13 | 14 | 15 | 16 | 17 | 18 |
| 19 | 20 | 21 | 22 | 23 | 24 | 25 |
| 26 | 27 | 28 | | | | |

| March | | | | | | |
|---|---|---|---|---|---|---|
| Su | M | Tu | W | Th | F | Sa |
| | | | 1 | 2 | 3 | 4 |
| 5 | 6 | 7 | 8 | 9 | 10 | 11 |
| 12 | 13 | 14 | 15 | 16 | 17 | 18 |
| 19 | 20 | 21 | 22 | 23 | 24 | 25 |
| 26 | 27 | 28 | 29 | 30 | 31 | |

## Your Parish Is the Curriculum

The next step in implementing a faith formation plan for each of your seekers is to identify where your parish is pursuing its apostolic vocation in each of the areas of Christian life described in RCIA 75. Where does your parish excel in the areas of word, community, worship, and witness?

Once you have identified your parish's areas of excellence, then prayerfully match those areas with the responses the seeker has given to the five questions. The formation for each seeker then becomes a process of immersion into the areas of parish life that will most effectively meet the needs of that seeker.

For example, let's say that one of your seekers focused on the need to know more about who God is and has expressed a desire to learn to pray. What are some of the ways your parish contemplates the mystery of God and offers prayer? In a typical parish, in addition to Sunday Mass, some activities might include:

- rosary group
- adoration
- Stations of the Cross
- men's prayer breakfast
- seasonal reconciliation services
- prayer before meals
- prayer before bed
- faith-sharing group
- prayer shawl ministry
- women's spirituality group
- bereavement support group
- seasonal evening prayer
- Taizé prayer
- novenas

If the seeker's sponsor is already participating in some of these prayer experiences, the sponsor can simply take the seeker to the prayer event. If the sponsor is not participating in any of these, you may need to consider whether the person is an appropriate choice for being a sponsor. However, you can ask someone from the rosary group or the prayer shawl ministry to accompany the seeker to their next gathering.

Make a similar list of activities your parish engages in for all the areas the seeker will need to learn about in order to accomplish the goals he or she identified in your inquiry sessions.

So a typical month of catechesis might look like this:

*Week 1*

- Sunday Mass with dismissal
- Formal **catechetical session** with catechumens and sponsors (separate from dismissal)

*Week 2*

- Sunday Mass with dismissal
- Sponsors take catechumens to a parish **small group**
- Informal mystagogical reflection with catechumens after the event (possibly facilitated by the sponsors)

*Week 3*

- Sunday Mass with dismissal
- Sponsors take catechumens to parishioner homes for **dinner**; try to have the catechumens in different parishioners' homes for dinner once a month or at least every other month
- Informal mystagogical reflection with catechumens during or after dinner (possibly facilitated by the sponsors)

*Week 4*

- Sunday Mass with dismissal

- Sponsors take catechumens to a parish **committee**

- Informal mystagogical reflection with catechumens after the event (possibly facilitated by the sponsors)

This is simply a suggested template, and you don't have to follow this exact pattern each month. Using your parish calendar as a guide, create a catechetical plan for your catechumens. See the model calendar in appendix 1 as a guide.

| Week | Date | Parish activity | Week | Date | Parish activity |
|------|------|-----------------|------|------|-----------------|
| 1 | | | 27 | | |
| 2 | | | 28 | | |
| 3 | | | 29 | | |
| 4 | | | 30 | | |
| 5 | | | 31 | | |
| 6 | | | 32 | | |
| 7 | | | 33 | | |
| 8 | | | 34 | | |
| 9 | | | 35 | | |
| 10 | | | 36 | | |
| 11 | | | 37 | | |
| 12 | | | 38 | | |
| 13 | | | 39 | | |
| 14 | | | 40 | | |
| 15 | | | 41 | | |
| 16 | | | 42 | | |
| 17 | | | 43 | | |
| 18 | | | 44 | | |
| 19 | | | 45 | | |
| 20 | | | 46 | | |
| 21 | | | 47 | | |
| 22 | | | 48 | | |
| 23 | | | 49 | | |
| 24 | | | 50 | | |
| 25 | | | 51 | | |
| 26 | | | 52 | | |

## Mystagogical Questions

For the informal mystagogical reflection, you can train the sponsors to ask in-depth questions of their catechumens about their experiences. You can also ask the catechumens to keep a journal of their experiences and discuss those during your monthly formal catechetical sessions.

Here are some examples of mystagogical reflection questions:

- What was your most memorable moment?

- What was your favorite part?

- What was a high point for you? What was boring or not engaging?

- How did this event make you feel?

- What did it mean to you?

- From your experience here, what have you learned about being a disciple of Christ?

- Did you experience the presence of God here? In what ways?

- Did God's word speak to you in this event? How?

- What did this experience tell you about God?

- What does it say about Christ?

- What in this event reminded you of something from the Bible or from our Christian traditions?

- From what you witnessed, how would you describe the mission or purpose of being a Catholic Christian?

- Based on what happened, how will you try to live differently this week?

You don't need to use these exact questions. Try to come up with at least six more of your own mystagogical questions the sponsors might ask. If you can think of more, even better!

## Two keys to success

To make a plan like this successful, there are two important points to keep in mind. First, this will not work in an abbreviated catechumenate that is squished into the fall and winter months before Lent—October through February, for example. A catechesis that is "complete in its coverage" (RCIA 75.1) will require at least one full liturgical year (see National Statutes for the Catechumenate, 6).

And secondly, this plan is not for baptized catechized candidates who want to complete their initiation (such as those preparing only for confirmation) or be received into full communion. If the candidates are completely uncatechized—meaning they have no relationship with or understanding of Jesus—then they "may participate in the elements of catechumenal formation so far as necessary and appropriate" (National Statutes for the Catechumenate, 31).

However, a great many of our baptized candidates have received *some* catechesis. Those folks should not be treated as catechumens. You will need to create a different, less intense, less lengthy process for most baptized candidates. Many times, they will need only some brief instruction in Catholic traditions that they may be unfamiliar with or may have some difficulty fully accepting.

---

I remember presenting these ideas to a group of people at an event several years ago. A woman right in front of me began to look more and more panicked. I asked her if she had a concern she wanted to share. She said, "Our parishioners are completely apathetic. If I had to rely on them to form the catechumens and candidates, no one would ever join the church!"

While I understand where that fear is coming from, it's just not true. All of our parishes are weak and fractured. All of us could do better. But if you live in a parish community that worships every Sunday, gathers for socials and missions, cares for one another in times of grief, and believes that Jesus died for our sins, you live in a community that is completely capable of initiating seekers into a life of discipleship. And there is no plan B. You cannot initiate seekers into your RCIA team. They are initiated into the Body of Christ, which, for better or worse, is manifest in and by your local parish.

So when we think about implementing a faith formation plan, it must have these components:

- Formation happens first of all in the parish community and is accomplished through the life of the parish.

- The primary formation event is the Sunday liturgy.

- Formation happens all year long and is marked by the liturgical cycle, during which the full mystery of Christ is revealed.

- Formation is integrated into the life of the seeker through a process of mystagogical reflection on his or her various encounters with Christ.

- These encounters cluster into four central markers of Christian discipleship:
    - A discipleship that is solidly rooted in the **word** of God
    - A life that is incorporated into the Christian **community**
    - A regular discipline of prayer and **worship**
    - A passion for **witness and service** in Christ's name

When you see your seekers consistently living out these four areas of Christian life, you will know they are ready for initiation. In the next chapter, we'll look more closely at exactly how we discern the readiness of the seekers to live as Christian disciples.

# Chapter 10

# Discernment for Readiness

The word *discernment* gets thrown around rather loosely sometimes, and the process of discernment gets fuzzy as a result. In relation to the RCIA, we can sometimes confuse "discernment" with "testing." When we do, a discernment interview with a catechumen becomes something like a final exam to see if he or she will "pass" and be able to be baptized.

## The Three Movements of Discernment

A true discernment process, however, does not start with the catechumen. It starts with us. According to Timothy M. Gallagher, OMV, in *The Discernment of Spirits*, a classic discernment process has three movements:

- be aware

- understand

- take action

## Be Aware

The first movement is that we have to be aware of what is going on. It is somewhat easy to understand what is going on outside of us. The harder challenge is to become aware of what is going on inside of us. In fact, we can sometimes focus on external activity as a way of distracting ourselves from paying attention to our interior thoughts and feelings. Gallagher says it takes real courage to focus on our spiritual awareness. He says spiritual awareness is the fundamental first step to all other aspects of discernment.

Spiritual awareness is more than just paying attention to what we are thinking or feeling. To be spiritually aware, we want to look into our heart-of-hearts, the very depths of our being. When we are discerning the readiness of an inquirer or a catechumen, does the thought of this person becoming a catechumen or being baptized fill you with joy? Or does it make you anxious and worried?

## Understand

The second step is to understand where the Spirit is leading us and leading the inquirer or catechumen. We can begin to identify where the Spirit is leading by noting specific, objective criteria for readiness.

The first place we will find that criteria is from the seeker. If we have done a good job of creating a faith formation plan based on responses to the five questions, we will have a set of objective criteria that the inquirers themselves have articulated.

We also want to take into account the criteria the church gives us. In the RCIA, there are two key places that speak about the criteria used for discernment:

- Paragraph 42 describes the prerequisites for inquirers wishing to celebrate the Rite of Acceptance into the Order of Catechumens.

- Paragraph 120 describes what is expected of the catechumens before they can celebrate the Rite of Election.

And then we sometimes also have our own conscious or unconscious checklists. For example, have the seekers come to enough sessions, have we covered enough doctrine, and are they living a morally acceptable lifestyle?

All of these objective criteria are useful but not sufficient. If you have been involved in initiation ministry for any length of time, you have probably encountered someone who met all the objective criteria, but you just didn't feel right in your gut about the person moving forward at that time.

Conversely, most of us know of at least one person who didn't seem to meet enough of the criteria before initiation, and he or she turned out to be an exemplary Christian. The point is, we cannot simply take out a checklist, like Santa before Christmas, and mark down who is "naughty" and "nice." Discernment through understanding is much more than making sure inquirers or catechumens cross off the things on their to-do lists. It is a deep, spiritual understanding of the will of God. We have to take the time to first be aware and then understand where it is God is leading us and the seekers.

## Take Action

Spiritual awareness and spiritual understanding, by themselves, are not discernment. For true discernment to take place, we have to take action based on our awareness and understanding. Once we have become aware and correctly interpreted the spiritual stirrings within us, the action we take based on those first two movements will result in true discernment.

Saint Ignatius used a binary method for determining what spiritual action to take: accept or reject. If Ignatius was aware and understood that a course of action was not of God, he rejected it. If he interpreted that it was part of the Lord's plan, he accepted it. Everything in a spiritual discernment process should be directed toward spiritual action—toward accepting or rejecting the course before us.

I sometimes worry that I am not qualified to say what the will of God is, even for myself. Perhaps you have that worry as well.

It is natural to think we may not be up to the task. But, in a sense, we don't have any other choice. At our baptism, we made promises (or they were made for us), and we frequently renew those promises. We promise to accept Christ and reject Satan. And in order to know which choice is an acceptance of Christ and which is a rejection of Satan, we have to be discerning. To be a disciple is to be a discerner.

Even so, if I worry that I am not able to discern God's will for myself, I worry much more when it comes to discerning God's will for others. How can I possibly know God's will for an inquirer? How can I know if God is leading the seeker to initiation at this moment?

It helps me to remember that a discernment process is a process. It is not a magic moment of blinding revelation.

It also helps when I remember that, in the catechumenate, I do not discern *for* the seekers. I discern *with* the seekers. Part of our job as RCIA leaders is to teach the seekers how to discern God's will for them. That means we have to enter into the three movements of discernment *with* them. And we have to discern constantly throughout their formation so they will learn how to accept or reject the course in front of them throughout their lives.

It also helps to remember that the whole community is involved in the discernment process: sponsors, family, friends, and other team members.

Finally, it helps me to remember that the first two movements of the discernment process are about deep listening to the Holy Spirit. We sometimes tell ourselves that it is difficult to know God's will. In reality, what is difficult is sitting still and listening. Because God is leading us quite clearly, if we pay attention. On the Fifteenth Sunday in Ordinary Time (Year C), we hear:

> For this command that I enjoin on you today
>     is not too mysterious and remote for you.
> It is not up in the sky, that you should say,
>     "Who will go up in the sky to get it for us
>     and tell us of it, that we may carry it out?"
> Nor is it across the sea, that you should say,

"Who will cross the sea to get it for us
and tell us of it, that we may carry it out?"
No, it is something very near to you,
already in your mouths and in your hearts;
you have only to carry it out. (Deut 30:11-14)

If we faithfully attend to the three spiritual movements—be aware, understand, take action—we can be confident we are always doing God's will.

Chapter 11

# The Ideal Catechist

In an ideal world, we catechists would not think of ourselves as those who are supplying knowledge to the inquirers. Instead, we would see ourselves as helpers who are confident in the inquirer's ability to come up with a fruitful faith formation plan for him- or herself. We would have a high regard for how the Holy Spirit has *already* gifted the inquirer, and we would believe in the power of the Holy Spirit to guide the inquirer on the path God has laid out. We would never want to or try to take the decision-making control away from the inquirer.

With every inquirer, we would strive for a true "encounter"— what Pope Francis calls an *encuentro*. The pope says that today "we are experiencing a profound *poverty of relationships*" (Message for the Celebration of the World Day of Peace, 5). To counter this impoverished experience, Pope Francis says "we must always be ready for encounter. . . . Because faith is an encounter with Jesus, and we must do what Jesus does: encounter others" (Address to the Pentecost Vigil with the Ecclesial Movements).

A true encounter would be a dialogue in which we listen more than we talk. The talk that we offer and the help that we offer would spring from the deep listening that we do. Our help would be tailored to the unique needs of each inquirer (see Knowles, *The Adult Learner*, 84).

And we would come to each encounter open to learning. We would expect that an encounter with every inquirer is an encounter with Christ. As such, we would expect to be changed just as Mary Magdalene was changed at the tomb when she encountered the "stranger" there.

## Spiritual Creatives

In any adult learning situation, discussion is crucial. This is especially true in the area of faith formation. Parker Palmer, in *The Courage to Teach*, describes how discussion enriches the learning experience and transforms not only the learner but also the teacher. In many RCIA settings, catechists have misunderstood their role. They tend to understand faith as a body of knowledge that is encapsulated in the Catechism. That body of knowledge is what Palmer calls the "Object" (102–3).

RCIA catechists, then, spend a lot of time becoming experts about the Object. Most of us don't think of ourselves as "experts," but the seekers see us that way. And when we create an environment in which our role is to tell the seekers everything they need to know about the Object, we then become the "Expert."

Our RCIA sessions then become a series of attempts to deliver to the nonexperts (who Palmer calls "Amateurs") enough knowledge to move the seekers from amateur status to expert status. In other words, we often see our job as RCIA catechists as making sure the seekers "know enough" before they can become Catholic.

Palmer illustrates this process, which he calls "Mythical objectivism," this way:

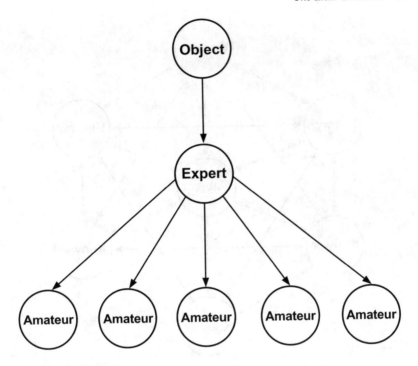

Mythical objectivism model

It is a myth that we, the experts, can effectively transmit an objective body of knowledge to the seekers. Indeed, there *is* an objective Truth by which we live our faith. That Truth is Jesus Christ. But as flawed humans, it is impossible for us to completely grasp or completely communicate who Jesus is to seekers. We can only invite seekers into the relationship we have with Jesus.

Palmer says that a better model for learning is to develop a "community of truth" (104–5). A community of truth is always in search of deeper meaning, better understanding, more disciplined living, and more passionate engagement with the Truth. In a community of truth model, Jesus becomes the Subject of our RCIA process. And all of us—catechists, seekers, sponsors, parishioners, and pastors—are equally engaged in the conversation about who Jesus is and how to live our lives as disciples.

Palmer illustrates the community of truth model this way:

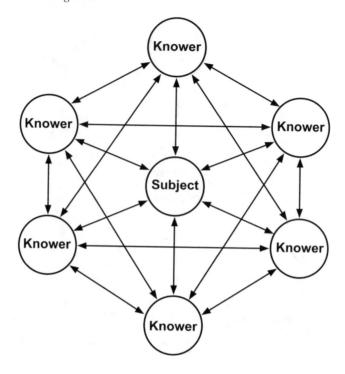

Community of truth model

A community of truth model of forming seekers will require new skills for many of us. One way to develop those skills is to take a lesson from one of the most successful learning organizations in the world: Google.

Google has discovered that a key to its success is "smart creatives." Google only hires smart creatives. A smart creative is someone who embodies the values of a modern-day business that intends to make a dent in the universe. The things that made workers and companies successful in the past are no longer useful, according to Google. Companies need to re-create themselves, and to do that, they need a new kind of worker. These new workers—the smart creatives—have unprecedented freedom and flexibility to execute the mission of the company.

Google executive chairman Eric Schmidt says:

> The primary objective [for businesses] today must be to increase the speed of the product development process and the quality of its output. . . . The defining characteristic of today's successful companies is the ability to continually deliver great products. (*How Google Works*, 17)

The church does not have a "great product," but it does have a great message. And our primary objective must be to increase the speed of the message delivery process and the quality of its output. (This is what Pope Francis means by evangelization.)

In order to do this, we have to form what I am calling "spiritual creatives"—disciples who have unprecedented freedom and flexibility to execute the mission of bringing the Gospel message to those on the peripheries of society.

Eric Schmidt lists the characteristics of a smart creative in his book, *How Google Works*. I have drawn on his structure and edited it with insights from Pope Francis's Joy of the Gospel to show what we should be looking for in ourselves, our colleagues, parishioners, and catechumens. This is what we should be looking for in spiritual creatives.

- The spiritual creative has **regular, renewing, personal encounters with Jesus Christ**, or at least an openness to letting Jesus encounter her. She does this unfailingly every day. She is comfortable with this risk because she knows the Lord never disappoints those who step out in faith (Joy of the Gospel, 3).

- **She is joyful.** Because she knows we live in messianic times, she insists that we all "shout aloud and sing for joy!" (Joy of the Gospel, 4).

- **She revels in life and its abundance.** This is her response to God's loving invitation: "My child, treat yourself well, according to your means. . . . Do not deprive yourself of the day's enjoyment" (Joy of the Gospel, 4).

- **She is a fully realized human being.** She takes to heart Pope Francis's exhortation that "we become fully human when we become more than human, when we let God bring us beyond ourselves in order to attain the fullest truth of our being" (Joy of the Gospel, 8).

- A spiritual creative is **dignified and fulfilled**. She is so because, in her humanity, she reaches out to others to seek their good (Joy of the Gospel, 9).

- **She is spiritually intense.** She lives life on a higher plane. She attains this higher plane of living by, paradoxically, letting go of the life she knows in order to risk her life for the sake of others. This commitment to daily sacrifice is a lodestar for her. Her guiding principle is that life grows in the measure that it is offered up for others (Joy of the Gospel, 10).

Not all our RCIA team members will have all of these characteristics, but they will have many of them. *You* have many of them. As parish leaders, we strive to discover or develop these traits in missionary disciples who will be sent out with the mission to tell the great story of Jesus to the world.

It is only by developing our skills as spiritual creatives that we will be able to communicate the truth of the Gospel. The message we have to deliver is not a message of objective conclusions. It is instead an invitation to dialogue within a community of truth. Palmer says:

> As we try to understand the subject [Jesus] in the community of truth, we enter into complex patterns of communication—sharing observations and interpretations, correcting and complementing each other, torn by conflict in this moment and joined by consensus in the next. The community of truth, far from being linear and static and hierarchical, is circular, interactive, and dynamic. (106)

If this model feels a little risky to you, that's because it is. There is safety and certainty in being able to say to seekers: "This is what the church teaches. End of story." But Jesus did not leave us with a finished text to be slavishly copied. He left us with a community of disciples—a community of truth—whose sole purpose was to invite others into that community, as weak and uncertain as it might be. It is that job, the job of inviting into community, that has been handed on to us to do today.

# Conclusion

# What Could Happen?

I began this book by introducing four seekers I met some years ago: Bill, Kevin, Adhi, and Alice. When I met them, I was a newcomer to the parish. I had no official status. The RCIA team did not know about my background in this ministry, and I don't think it would have mattered to them if they had known. In their eyes, I was a new volunteer and perhaps even something of a threat to "the way we've always done it."

Many times, we think change has to come from the top. And the "top" is always someone with more authority, more education, or more vision than we have. However, I think change happens more often when we begin to ask questions. Organizational development consultant Peter Block says the skill is getting the questions right. He writes:

> The traditional conversations that seek to explain, study, analyze, define tools, and express the desire to change others are interesting but not powerful. They actually are forms of wanting to maintain control. If we adhere to them, they become a limitation to the future, not a pathway.
>
> The future is brought into the present when citizens engage each other through questions of possibility, commitment, dissent, and gifts. *Questions open the door to the future and are more powerful than answers in that they demand engagement.* Engagement

in the right questions is what creates accountability. (*Community,* 101; emphasis added)

## Questions That Demand Engagement

The short story, "The Friday Everything Changed," by Anne Hart, perfectly describes the way in which the right question can open the door to the future and demand engagement.

Hart's story focuses on a single question that challenges the status quo, and in doing so, causes deep engagement in a school community. The hero of the story is young Alma Niles, a child who is constrained by layers of authority including long-standing tradition, her teacher, and the male privilege ascribed to boys over girls. One Friday, Alma decided to question the rule that getting water every Friday for the class was a boy's job. Getting water for the class was something of a rite of passage for young boys. Only the big boys were chosen, and younger boys would dream of growing strong enough to one day be chosen. Girls, of course, were never chosen.

Until that fateful Friday. On that day, Alma's teacher, Miss Ralston, picked two boys to fetch the water. Alma asked the right question: Why couldn't girls get the water?

Miss Ralston said nothing at all for a moment but just looked very hard at Alma, who had gone quite white with the shock of dropping such a bombshell.

After a long moment, when she finally spoke, Miss Ralston, instead of saying, "Why that's out of the question, Alma," threw a bombshell of her own: "I'll think about that," she said—as if, you knew, she would—"and I'll let you know next Friday."

The point of the story is not what Miss Ralston's ultimate decision would be. The point is that simply by asking the question, Alma had already crossed a boundary that had never before been breached. As soon as she did that, her life and the lives of everyone in the school changed.

The boys knew it right away, of course, as we all do when someone challenges a long-standing tradition. The boys felt threatened by Alma's question. If there was any question about girls carrying the water, the boys were compelled to do everything in their power to stop it. First, they tried to physically intimidate Alma, targeting her at lunchtime. And, when school resumed the next week, the bigger boys issued a ban against any girls playing on the school softball field during recess.

It was a difficult week for the girls. Some of them urged Alma to withdraw her inquiry about girls carrying the water so that things could go back to normal. But that was no longer possible. "Normal" had been forever changed by Alma's question. Even if she had folded, or if Miss Ralston had decided to enforce the traditional boys-only rule, Alma had already caused the entire school to imagine the possibility of a new future.

## Finding the Right Question

Finding the right question sometimes takes some exploration. The underlying question I started with, the one I first asked myself, is: Can a catechumenate process be driven by the needs of the seekers instead of my need to teach them what I know?

While that question was right for me, it didn't feel like the right question for the RCIA team in my new parish. As I got to know the team, and as I got to know the four seekers that year, I pondered a different question: Why does Bill have to go through our entire process from September through Easter Vigil?

Remember, Bill was the evangelical Protestant who had memorized much of the Bible and had met with more than two dozen priests by the time he showed up to this parish, asking to become Catholic. I wondered what would happen if I focused my question on Bill's process. I wondered if it would have the same disruptive effect on the parish that Alma's question had on her school.

As soon as I raised the question, I felt I had gotten it wrong. There was immediate and strong resistance from everyone on the team. But then I remembered that dissent is part of the process of imagining a new future. Peter Block writes:

> Creating space for dissent is the way diversity gets valued in
> the world. Inviting dissent into the conversation is how we show
> respect for a wide range of beliefs. It honors the Bohr maxim
> that for every great idea, the opposite idea is also true. (130)

So I kept asking. Over several more meetings, I wondered out loud how Bill and the parish might benefit from a simpler, shorter process. At one point, I suggested we ask Bill what he wanted (by using the five questions I've outlined in this book).

Eventually, with the support of the pastor and a couple of team members who had begun to imagine a new future, we did decide to receive Bill into full communion "ahead of schedule." But it was not a harmonious decision. For months afterward, some team members kept expressing regret that Bill had missed out on the full process and were vowing to never let anything like that happen again.

But even if the decision had gone the other way and Bill had to endure months of classes on basic Catholic doctrine—many of which he could have taught—I started to hope that my question had forever changed that RCIA team. I was cautiously optimistic that it had caused them to imagine a new future.

## What Is Your New Future?

My hope is that in writing this book, I've caused *you* to imagine a new future. This matters for you because you are never going to have exact duplicates of Bill, Kevin, Adhi, and Alice in your parish. Your RCIA team will never exactly mirror mine. Your pastor will never make the same decisions or have the same approach to RCIA as mine.

And, as you imagine a new future and as you begin to ask questions, you will probably meet resistance. That is okay. As Peter Block suggests, dissent creates an opening for commitment. When dissent is expressed, we should not feel compelled to solve the problem, defend ourselves, or explain anything. We should just listen.

## Everyone Has Gifts—Even Those Who Disagree with Us

The most difficult part for me in this entire process is exactly that—just listening to those who disagree with me. However, if I believe that the Holy Spirit sends us seekers who are already gifted and already on a path to conversion—and I have to first listen to them and recognize their giftedness—the same is true with dissenters. The Holy Spirit has put them in my life for a reason. What gifts do they have that I do not see? What insight do they have that I don't have access to? What message do they have that I need to hear?

Block writes:

> The communal possibility comes into being through individual public declarations of possibility. Much the same as witnessing in religious gatherings. Though every possibility begins as an individual declaration, it gains power and impacts community when made public. The community possibility is not the aggregation of individual possibilities. Nor is it a negotiation or agreement on common possibility. The communal possibility is that space or porous container where a collective exists for the realization of all the possibilities of its members. This is the real meaning of a restorative community. It is that place where all possibilities can come alive, and they come alive at the moment they are announced. (125)

Christian community does not exist so that the person with the most authority, education, vision, or charisma gets his way. It exists "for the realization of all the possibilities of its members."

Or, as St. Paul put it:

> There are different kinds of spiritual gifts but the same Spirit; there are different forms of services but the same Lord; there are different workings but the same God who produces all of them in everyone. . . . If [one] part suffers, all the parts suffer with it; if one part is honored, all the parts share its joy. (1 Cor 12:4-7, 26)

## Next Steps

If you want to cause real change in your seekers and in your parish (and in yourself), you have to ask the right questions. I suggest you start with the five I have given you in this book. And start with yourself.

Ask yourself, in regard to your ministry as an RCIA leader in your parish:

1. Where have you been?

2. Where are you now?

3. Where do you want to get to?

4. How are you going to get to where you want to go?

5. How will you know you have arrived?

Then ask everyone else on your RCIA team to answer the same five questions.

If he is open to it, ask your pastor to do the same.

Just asking yourself these questions will cause change. It will change you, and that in turn will change your team. And that will change your parish.

Then, once you have done that and once you have gotten everyone on your team to do the same, ask yourselves one more question:

What could happen if we did this with our very next seeker?

That is the right question.

------

I eventually moved on to another parish. However, I still wondered if my questioning of the initiation process at the parish where I met those four seekers had really helped the RCIA team imagine a new future. Or, had I just been an irritant?

Then, a few years later, I was having breakfast at a neighborhood restaurant. A woman started to walk toward me, and I recognized her as one of the loudest dissenters from my previous RCIA team. I felt a knot in my stomach, worried she might have more "dissent" she wanted to share with me.

Quite to the contrary, she started profusely thanking me. She told me how much better the initiation process was now at her parish. She said it had been my questioning of the status quo that had begun the process of the RCIA team finding a new way of initiating seekers.

I count that encounter as a gift of the Holy Spirit to encourage me to keep searching for the right question. And I also realize that every situation won't end with such a tidy, gratifying solution. The challenge for me and for all of us committed to this ministry is not to find the right answers. It is to seek the right questions.

# Appendix 1

# A Model Calendar for a Formation Plan for Seekers

This is an example of how to use the activities of the parish for a year-round formation process. It starts in October of one year and concludes in October of the following year. You can start in any month of the year and extend the formation for as long as your seekers require, "several years if necessary" (RCIA 76). Seekers who are somewhat catechized already and who do not require extensive formation might participate in this kind of process for only a few months.

Some form of parish activity is scheduled once a week. You may need to schedule fewer activities, depending on the needs of your individual seekers. Your parish may not have all of the activities I have used as examples in this plan. In that case, substitute activities your parish does have.

Formal catechetical sessions are scheduled once a month. You may need more or fewer, depending upon the individual needs of your seekers.

## October
*Week 1*

- Sunday Mass with Rite of Acceptance and dismissal of catechumens, followed by faith sharing
- Catechetical session with catechumens and sponsors

*Week 2*

- Sunday Mass and dismissal of catechumens, followed by fellowship
- After Mass, catechumens and sponsors are invited to participate in the Small Christian Community faith sharing
- Catechumens and sponsors are invited to dinner at parishioners' homes

*Week 3*

- Sunday Mass and dismissal of catechumens, followed by faith sharing
- Catechumens and sponsors are invited to attend the Parish Council Meeting

*Week 4*

- Sunday Mass and dismissal of catechumens, followed by faith sharing
- Catechumens and sponsors are invited to attend the Knights of Columbus Halloween Dance

# November

*Week 1*

- All Saints' Day Mass and dismissal of catechumens, followed by faith sharing
- Sunday Mass and dismissal of catechumens, followed by faith sharing
- Catechumens and sponsors are invited to participate in the Just Faith meeting

*Week 2*

- Sunday Mass and dismissal of catechumens, followed by faith sharing
- Catechetical session with catechumens and sponsors

- Catechumens and sponsors are invited to dinner at parishioners' homes

### Week 3

- Sunday Mass and dismissal of catechumens, followed by faith sharing
- Catechumens and sponsors are invited to participate in the choir rehearsal and sing with them at the Christ the King Sunday Mass

### Week 4

- Christ the King Sunday Mass and dismissal of catechumens, followed by faith sharing
- Catechumens and sponsors are invited to help decorate the church for Advent

### Week 5

- First Sunday of Advent Mass and dismissal of catechumens, followed by faith sharing
- Catechumens and sponsors are invited to participate in the Liturgy Committee meeting

# December

### Week 1

- Second Sunday of Advent Mass and dismissal of catechumens, followed by faith sharing
- Catechetical session with catechumens and sponsors
- Immaculate Conception Holy Day Mass and dismissal of catechumens, followed by fellowship

### Week 2

- Third Sunday of Advent Mass and dismissal of catechumens, followed by faith sharing

- Catechumens and sponsors are invited to dinner at parishioners' homes

### Week 3

- Fourth Sunday of Advent Mass and dismissal of catechumens, followed by faith sharing
- Christmas Mass and dismissal of catechumens, followed by fellowship

### Week 4

- Sunday Mass and dismissal of catechumens, followed by faith sharing

## January

### Week 1

- Mary the Mother of God Holy Day Mass and dismissal of catechumens, followed by fellowship
- Sunday Mass and dismissal of catechumens, followed by faith sharing

### Week 2

- Sunday Mass and dismissal of catechumens, followed by faith sharing
- Catechetical session with catechumens and sponsors
- Catechumens and sponsors are invited to dinner at parishioners' homes

### Week 3

- Sunday Mass and dismissal of catechumens, followed by faith sharing
- Catechumens and sponsors are invited to attend a parish funeral (Note that this obviously cannot be scheduled a year ahead of time; the idea is to make sure the catechumens participate in a funeral liturgy as part of their formation.)

*Week 4*

- Sunday Mass (with possible Rite of Acceptance for new inquirers) and dismissal of catechumens, followed by faith sharing
- Catechumens and sponsors are invited to assist with parish food pantry

*Week 5*

- Sunday Mass and dismissal of catechumens, followed by faith sharing
- Catechumens and sponsors are invited to attend Sacramental Preparation Parents' Meeting

# February
*Week 1*

- Sunday Mass and dismissal of catechumens, followed by faith sharing
- Catechumens and sponsors are invited to participate in Valentine's Day Dinner Dance

*Week 2*

- Sunday Mass with rite of sending for those who will become elect and dismissal of catechumens, followed by faith sharing (Note that not all of the catechumens will necessarily become elect; only those who are ready to be initiated this Easter.)
- Catechetical session with catechumens and sponsors
- Ash Wednesday Mass and dismissal of catechumens, followed by faith sharing

*Week 3*

- First Sunday of Lent Mass and dismissal of catechumens, followed by faith sharing
- Catechumens and sponsors are invited to dinner at parishioners' homes

*Week 4*

- Second Sunday of Lent Mass and dismissal of catechumens, followed by faith sharing
- Catechumens and sponsors are invited to participate in parish Stations of the Cross

# March

*Week 1*

- Third Sunday of Lent Mass with First Scrutiny for the elect and dismissal of catechumens, followed by faith sharing
- Catechumens and sponsors participate in parish reconciliation service (catechumens cannot receive the sacrament, but they can participate)

*Week 2*

- Fourth Sunday of Lent Mass with Second Scrutiny for the elect and dismissal of catechumens, followed by faith sharing
- Catechetical session with catechumens and sponsors (elect and their godparents participate in a Lenten retreat)
- Catechumens and sponsors are invited to dinner at parishioners' homes

*Week 3*

- Fifth Sunday of Lent Mass with Third Scrutiny for the elect and dismissal of catechumens, followed by faith sharing
- Catechumens and sponsors are invited to participate in parish Lenten Small Group Reflection

*Week 4*

- Palm Sunday Mass and dismissal of catechumens, followed by faith sharing
- Holy Thursday Mass and dismissal of catechumens, followed by faith sharing

- Catechumens and sponsors are invited to participate in the parish Stations of the Cross
- Good Friday liturgy and dismissal of catechumens (prior to the universal prayer), followed by prayer around the cross
- Elect and godparents participate in Holy Saturday Preparation Rites

## Easter Vigil
*Week 5*

- Easter Sunday Mass and dismissal of catechumens, followed by fellowship
- Neophytes, godparents, catechumens, and sponsors are invited to participate in the parish Easter Banquet

## April
*Week 1*

- Second Sunday of Easter Mass with testimony from a neophyte and dismissal of catechumens, followed by faith sharing
- Catechumens and sponsors, and neophytes and godparents, are invited to dinner at parishioners' homes

*Week 2*

- Third Sunday of Easter Mass with testimony from a neophyte and dismissal of catechumens, followed by faith sharing
- Catechetical session with catechumens and sponsors

*Week 3*

- Fourth Sunday of Easter Mass with testimony from a neophyte and dismissal of catechumens, followed by faith sharing
- Catechumens and sponsors are invited to attend the monthly MOMS ("Mothers on Mission") meeting

*Week 4*

- Fifth Sunday of Easter Mass with testimony from a neophyte or godparent and dismissal of catechumens, followed by faith sharing
- Catechumens and sponsors are invited to attend the monthly Men's Ministry Meeting

# May

*Week 1*

- Sixth Sunday of Easter Mass with testimony from a neophyte or godparent and dismissal of catechumens
- After Mass, catechumens and sponsors participate in the parish infant baptism liturgy
- Catechumens and sponsors are invited to attend the Separated and Divorced Meeting
- If Ascension is celebrated on Thursday, Ascension Thursday Mass and dismissal of catechumens, followed by fellowship

*Week 2*

- Seventh Sunday of Easter or Ascension Sunday Mass with testimony from a neophyte or godparent and dismissal of catechumens, followed by faith sharing
- Catechetical session with catechumens and sponsors
- Catechumens and sponsors, and neophytes and godparents, are invited to dinner at parishioners' homes

*Week 3*

- Pentecost Sunday Mass with testimony from a neophyte or godparent and dismissal of catechumens, followed by fellowship
- Catechumens and sponsors are invited to participate in a parish Bible study meeting

*Week 4*

- Most Holy Trinity Sunday Mass and dismissal of catechumens, followed by faith sharing
- Catechumens and sponsors are invited to attend a parish wedding (Note that this obviously cannot be scheduled a year ahead of time; the idea is to make sure the catechumens participate in a wedding liturgy as part of their formation.)

# June

*Week 1*

- Most Holy Body and Blood of Christ Sunday Mass and dismissal of catechumens, followed by faith sharing
- Catechumens and sponsors invited to an hour of prayer before the Blessed Sacrament

*Week 2*

- Sunday Mass and dismissal of catechumens, followed by faith sharing
- Catechumens and sponsors invited to participate in Communion to the homebound

*Week 3*

- Sunday Mass (with possible Rite of Acceptance for new inquirers) and dismissal of catechumens, followed by faith sharing
- Catechetical session with catechumens and sponsors
- Catechumens and sponsors are invited to dinner at parishioners' homes

*Week 4*

- Sunday Mass and dismissal of catechumens, followed by faith sharing

- Catechumens and sponsors are invited to the diocesan cele-bration for neophytes

# July

*Week 1*

- Sunday Mass and dismissal of catechumens, followed by faith sharing
- Catechumens and sponsors invited to the parish Fourth of July picnic

*Week 2*

- Sunday Mass and dismissal of catechumens, followed by faith sharing
- Catechumens and sponsors invited to attend the parish Can-cer Survivors Meeting

*Week 3*

- Sunday Mass and dismissal of catechumens, followed by faith sharing
- Catechetical session with catechumens and sponsors
- Catechumens and sponsors are invited to attend the parish St. Vincent de Paul Society meeting

*Week 4*

- Sunday Mass and dismissal of catechumens, followed by faith sharing
- Catechumens and sponsors are invited to attend Summer Theology on Tap

*Week 5*

- Sunday Mass and dismissal of catechumens, followed by faith sharing
- Catechumens and sponsors are invited to attend the Women's Club meeting

# August
*Week 1*

- Sunday Mass and dismissal of catechumens, followed by faith sharing
- Catechumens and sponsors invited to attend the parish softball game

*Week 2*

- Sunday Mass and dismissal of catechumens, followed by faith sharing
- Catechetical session with catechumens and sponsors
- Assumption of Mary holy day Mass and dismissal of catechumens, followed by faith sharing

*Week 3*

- Sunday Mass and dismissal of catechumens, followed by faith sharing
- Catechumens and sponsors are invited to dinner at parishioners' homes

*Week 4*

- Sunday Mass and dismissal of catechumens, followed by faith sharing
- Catechumens and sponsors are invited to participate in the parish Rosary Prayer Group

# September
*Week 1*

- Sunday Mass and dismissal of catechumens, followed by faith sharing
- Catechumens and sponsors are invited to participate in the parish Charismatic Prayer Group Meeting

*Week 2*

- Sunday Mass and dismissal of catechumens, followed by faith sharing
- Catechetical session with catechumens and sponsors
- Catechumens and sponsors are invited to dinner at parishioners' homes

*Week 3*

- Sunday Mass and dismissal of catechumens, followed by faith sharing
- Catechumens and sponsors are invited to attend the parish Youth Group Meeting

*Week 4*

- Sunday Mass and dismissal of catechumens, followed by faith sharing
- Catechumens and sponsors are invited to attend the parish Ladies Auxiliary Chili Cook-Off Dinner

## October

*Week 1*

- Sunday Mass (with possible Rite of Acceptance for new inquirers) and dismissal of catechumens, followed by faith sharing
- Catechetical session with catechumens and sponsors
- Catechumens and sponsors are invited to dinner at parishioners' homes

# Appendix 2

# Goal-Setting Worksheet for Becoming a Disciple

List four characteristics you believe would show evidence of being an excellent disciple of Jesus Christ. For each characteristic, list three specific behaviors (things you would see or hear a person do) that tell you that they have that particular characteristic.

Use this worksheet to evaluate your progress toward your goal of becoming a disciple. Try as best you can to make sure you are doing all these behaviors consistently throughout your formation process.

—Adapted from a process by Laurie Krupp

| 1) Characteristic | a) Behavior |
|---|---|
| | b) Behavior |
| | c) Behavior |
| 2) Characteristic | a) Behavior |
| | b) Behavior |
| | c) Behavior |
| 3) Characteristic | a) Behavior |
| | b) Behavior |
| | c) Behavior |
| 4) Characteristic | a) Behavior |
| | b) Behavior |
| | c) Behavior |

# Appendix 3

# Catholic Prayers

## The Sign of the Cross
In the name of the Father,
and of the Son,
and of the Holy Spirit. Amen.

## Our Father
Our Father, who art in heaven,
hallowed be thy name;
thy kingdom come,
thy will be done
on earth as it is in heaven.
Give us this day our daily bread,
and forgive us our trespasses,
as we forgive those who trespass against us;
and lead us not into temptation,
but deliver us from evil.

## The Hail Mary
Hail, Mary, full of grace,
the Lord is with thee.
Blessed art thou among women

and blessed is the fruit of thy womb, Jesus.
Holy Mary, Mother of God,
pray for us sinners
now and at the hour of our death.
Amen.

## Grace Before Meals

Bless us, O Lord, and these thy gifts, which we are about to receive from thy bounty, through Christ our Lord. Amen.

## Glory Be (Doxology)

Glory be to the Father
and to the Son
and to the Holy Spirit,
as it was in the beginning
is now, and ever shall be
world without end. Amen.

## The Apostles' Creed

I believe in God
the Father almighty,
Creator of heaven and earth.
And in Jesus Christ, his only Son, our Lord,
who was conceived by the Holy Spirit,
born of the Virgin Mary,
suffered under Pontius Pilate,
was crucified, died, and was buried.
He descended into hell;
the third day he rose again from the dead;

he ascended into heaven,
and sits at the right hand of God the Father almighty,
from thence he shall come to judge the living and the dead.

I believe in the Holy Spirit,
the holy Catholic Church,
the communion of saints,
the forgiveness of sins,
the resurrection of the body
and life everlasting. Amen.


## Angel of God

Angel of God,
my guardian dear,
to whom God's love commits me here,
ever this day be at my side,
to light and guard, to rule and guide.
Amen.


## Prayer to the Holy Spirit

Come, Holy Spirit, fill the hearts of your faithful.
And kindle in them the fire of your love.
Send forth your Spirit and they shall be created.
And you will renew the face of the earth.

Lord,
by the light of the Holy Spirit
you have taught the hearts of your faithful.
In the same Spirit
help us to relish what is right
and always rejoice in your consolation.
We ask this through Christ our Lord.
Amen.


## Morning Offering

My God, I offer you my prayers,
works, joys and sufferings of this day

in union with the holy sacrifice of the Mass throughout the
world.
I offer them for all the intentions of your Son's Sacred Heart,
for the salvation of souls, reparation for sin,
and the reunion of Christians.
Amen.


## Hail, Holy Queen

Hail, holy Queen, Mother of mercy:
Hail, our life, our sweetness and our hope.
To you do we cry, poor banished children of Eve.
To you do we send up our sighs,
mourning and weeping in this valley of tears.
Turn then, most gracious advocate,
your eyes of mercy toward us;
and after this our exile
show unto us the blessed fruit of your womb, Jesus
O clement, O loving, O sweet Virgin Mary.


## Litany of the Sacred Heart of Jesus

| | |
|---|---|
| Lord, have mercy | Lord, have mercy |
| Christ, have mercy | Christ, have mercy |
| Lord, have mercy | Lord, have mercy |
| | |
| God our Father in heaven | have mercy on us |
| God the Son, Redeemer of the world | have mercy on us |
| God the Holy Spirit | have mercy on us |
| Holy Trinity, one God | have mercy on us |
| | |
| Heart of Jesus, Son of the eternal Father | have mercy on us |
| Heart of Jesus, formed by the Holy Spirit in the womb of the Virgin Mother | have mercy on us |
| Heart of Jesus, one with the eternal Word | have mercy on us |
| Heart of Jesus, infinite in majesty | have mercy on us |

Heart of Jesus, holy temple of God                                    have mercy on us
Heart of Jesus, tabernacle of the Most High        have mercy on us
Heart of Jesus, house of God and
    gate of heaven                                               have mercy on us
Heart of Jesus, aflame with love for us                have mercy on us
Heart of Jesus, source of justice and love          have mercy on us
Heart of Jesus, full of goodness and love           have mercy on us
Heart of Jesus, wellspring of all virtue               have mercy on us
Heart of Jesus, worthy of all praise                      have mercy on us
Heart of Jesus, King and center of all hearts     have mercy on us
Heart of Jesus, treasurehouse of wisdom
    and knowledge                                              have mercy on us
Heart of Jesus, in whom there dwells
    the fullness of God                                        have mercy on us
Heart of Jesus, in whom the
    Father is well pleased                                   have mercy on us
Heart of Jesus, from whose fullness
    we have all received                                      have mercy on us
Heart of Jesus, desire of the eternal hills          have mercy on us
Heart of Jesus, patient and full of mercy            have mercy on us
Heart of Jesus, generous to all
    who turn to you                                             have mercy on us
Heart of Jesus, fountain of life and holiness       have mercy on us
Heart of Jesus, atonement for our sins               have mercy on us
Heart of Jesus, overwhelmed with insults          have mercy on us
Heart of Jesus, broken for our sins                      have mercy on us
Heart of Jesus, obedient even to death              have mercy on us
Heart of Jesus, pierced by a lance                      have mercy on us
Heart of Jesus, source of all consolation           have mercy on us
Heart of Jesus, our life and resurrection            have mercy on us
Heart of Jesus, our peace and reconciliation      have mercy on us
Heart of Jesus, victim of our sins                        have mercy on us
Heart of Jesus, salvation of all
    who trust in you                                           have mercy on us
Heart of Jesus, hope of all who die in you          have mercy on us
Heart of Jesus, delight of all the saints              have mercy on us

Lamb of God, you take away
    the sins of the world                 have mercy on us
Lamb of God, you take away
    the sins of the world                 have mercy on us
Lamb of God, you take away
    the sins of the world                 have mercy on us

Jesus, gentle and humble of heart.     Touch our hearts and
make them like your own.

Let us pray. Father, we rejoice in the gifts of love we have
received from the heart of Jesus your Son. Open our hearts to
share his life and continue to bless us with his love. We ask this
in the name of Jesus the Lord. Amen.

## Litany of the Saints

Lord, have mercy                 Lord, have mercy
Christ, have mercy              Christ, have mercy
Lord, have mercy                 Lord, have mercy

Holy Mary, Mother of God,          pray for us
Saint Michael,                   pray for us
Holy Angels of God,              pray for us
Saint John the Baptist,           pray for us
Saint Joseph,                    pray for us
Saint Peter and Saint Paul,        pray for us
Saint Andrew,                   pray for us
Saint John,                     pray for us
Saint Mary Magdalene,          pray for us
Saint Stephen,                  pray for us
Saint Ignatius of Antioch,         pray for us
Saint Lawrence,                pray for us

Saint Perpetua and Saint Felicity,                                pray for us
Saint Agnes,                                                      pray for us
Saint Gregory,                                                    pray for us
Saint Augustine,                                                  pray for us
Saint Athanasius,                                                 pray for us
Saint Basil,                                                      pray for us
Saint Martin,                                                     pray for us
Saint Benedict,                                                   pray for us
Saint Francis and Saint Dominic,                                  pray for us
Saint Francis Xavier,                                             pray for us
Saint John Vianney,                                               pray for us
Saint Catherine of Siena,                                         pray for us
Saint Teresa of Jesus,                                            pray for us
All holy men and women, Saints of God,                            pray for us

Lord, be merciful                        Lord, deliver us, we pray.
From all evil,                           Lord, deliver us, we pray.
From every sin,                          Lord, deliver us, we pray.
From everlasting death,                  Lord, deliver us, we pray.
By your Incarnation,                     Lord, deliver us, we pray.
By your Death and Resurrection,          Lord, deliver us, we pray.
By the outpouring of the Holy Spirit,    Lord, deliver us, we pray.

Be merciful to us sinners,        Lord, we ask you, hear our prayer.
Bring these chosen ones
    to new birth through
    the grace of Baptism,         Lord, we ask you, hear our prayer.
Make this font holy by
    your grace for the new
    birth of your children,       Lord, we ask you, hear our prayer.
Jesus, Son of the living God,     Lord, we ask you, hear our prayer.

Christ hear us.                                    Christ, hear us.
Christ, graciously hear us.            Christ, graciously hear us.

# Litany of the Holy Name of Jesus

| | |
|---|---|
| Lord, have mercy | Lord, have mercy |
| Christ, have mercy | Christ, have mercy |
| Lord, have mercy | Lord, have mercy |
| | |
| God our Father in heaven | have mercy on us |
| God the Son, Redeemer of the world | have mercy on us |
| God the Holy Spirit | have mercy on us |
| Holy Trinity, one God | have mercy on us |
| | |
| Jesus, Son of the living God | have mercy on us |
| Jesus, splendor of the Father | have mercy on us |
| Jesus, brightness of everlasting light | have mercy on us |
| Jesus, king of glory | have mercy on us |
| Jesus, dawn of justice | have mercy on us |
| Jesus, Son of the Virgin Mary | have mercy on us |
| Jesus, worthy of our love | have mercy on us |
| Jesus, worthy of our wonder | have mercy on us |
| Jesus, mighty God | have mercy on us |
| Jesus, father of the world to come | have mercy on us |
| Jesus, prince of peace | have mercy on us |
| Jesus, all-powerful | have mercy on us |
| Jesus, pattern of patience | have mercy on us |
| Jesus, model of obedience | have mercy on us |
| Jesus, gentle and humble of heart | have mercy on us |
| Jesus, lover of chastity | have mercy on us |
| Jesus, lover of us all | have mercy on us |
| Jesus, God of peace | have mercy on us |
| Jesus, author of life | have mercy on us |
| Jesus, model of goodness | have mercy on us |
| Jesus, seeker of souls | have mercy on us |
| Jesus, our God | have mercy on us |
| Jesus, our refuge | have mercy on us |
| Jesus, father of the poor | have mercy on us |
| Jesus, treasure of the faithful | have mercy on us |
| Jesus, Good Shepherd | have mercy on us |

| | |
|---|---|
| Jesus, the true light | have mercy on us |
| Jesus, eternal wisdom | have mercy on us |
| Jesus, infinite goodness | have mercy on us |
| Jesus, our way and our life | have mercy on us |
| Jesus, joy of angels | have mercy on us |
| Jesus, King of patriarchs | have mercy on us |
| Jesus, Teacher of apostles | have mercy on us |
| Jesus, Master of evangelists | have mercy on us |
| Jesus, courage of martyrs | have mercy on us |
| Jesus, light of confessors | have mercy on us |
| Jesus, purity of virgins | have mercy on us |
| Jesus, crown of all saints | have mercy on us |

| | |
|---|---|
| Lord, be merciful | Jesus, save your people |
| From all evil | Jesus, save your people |
| From every sin | Jesus, save your people |
| From the snares of the devil | Jesus, save your people |
| From your anger | Jesus, save your people |
| From the spirit of infidelity | Jesus, save your people |
| From everlasting death | Jesus, save your people |
| From neglect of your Holy Spirit | Jesus, save your people |
| By the mystery of your Incarnation | Jesus, save your people |
| By your birth | Jesus, save your people |
| By your childhood | Jesus, save your people |
| By your hidden life | Jesus, save your people |
| By your public ministry | Jesus, save your people |
| By your agony and crucifixion | Jesus, save your people |
| By your abandonment | Jesus, save your people |
| By your grief and sorrow | Jesus, save your people |
| By your death and burial | Jesus, save your people |
| By your rising to new life | Jesus, save your people |
| By your return in glory to the Father | Jesus, save your people |
| By your gift of the Holy Eucharist | Jesus, save your people |
| By your joy and glory | Jesus, save your people |

| | |
|---|---|
| Christ, hear us | Christ, hear us |
| Lord Jesus, hear our prayer | Lord Jesus, hear our prayer |

Lamb of God, you take away the
   sins of the world                          have mercy on us
Lamb of God, you take away the
   sins of the world                          have mercy on us
Lamb of God, you take away the
   sins of the world                          have mercy on us

Let us pray. Lord, may we who honor the holy name of Jesus
enjoy his friendship in this life and be filled with eternal joy in
the Kingdom where he lives and reigns forever and ever. Amen.

## Canticle of the Sun

Be praised, my Lord,
For all your creatures,
And first for brother sun,
Who makes the day bright and luminous.
He is beautiful and radiant
With great splendor
He is the image of You,
Most high.
Be praised, my Lord,
For sister moon and the stars.
You placed them in the sky,
So bright and twinkling.

## Holy Spirit Prayer of Saint Augustine

Breathe in me, O Holy Spirit,
That my thoughts may all be holy.
Act in me, O Holy Spirit,
That my work, too, may be holy.
Draw my heart, O Holy Spirit,
That I love but what is holy.
Strengthen me, O Holy Spirit,
To defend all that is holy.
Guard me, then, O Holy Spirit,
That I always may be holy.

## Prayer of Saint Francis (Peace Prayer)

Lord, make me an instrument of your peace:
where there is hatred, let me sow love;
where there is injury, pardon;
where there is doubt, faith;
where there is despair, hope;
where there is darkness, light;
where there is sadness, joy.

O divine Master, grant that I may not so much seek
to be consoled as to console,
to be understood as to understand,
to be loved as to love.

For it is in giving that we receive,
it is in pardoning that we are pardoned,
it is in dying that we are born to eternal life.
Amen.

## Act of Contrition

My God,
I am sorry for my sins with all my heart.
In choosing to do wrong
and failing to do good,
I have sinned against you
whom I should love above all things.
I firmly intend, with your help,
to do penance,
to sin no more,
and to avoid whatever leads me to sin.
Our Savior Jesus Christ
suffered and died for us.
In his name, my God, have mercy.

# Prayer to Saint Michael the Archangel

Saint Michael Archangel,
defend us in battle,
be our protection against the wickedness and snares of the devil;
may God rebuke him, we humbly pray;
and do thou, O Prince of the heavenly host,
by the power of God,
cast into hell Satan and all the evil spirits
who prowl through the world seeking the ruin of souls.
Amen.

# Bibliography

Block, Peter. *Community: The Structure of Belonging*. San Francisco, CA: Berrett-Koehler, 2009.

Francis, Pope. The Joy of the Gospel (*Evangelii Gaudium*). Apostolic Exhortation on the Proclamation of the Gospel in Today's World. November 24, 2013. http://w2.vatican.va/content/francesco/en/apost_exhortations /documents/papa-francesco_esortazione-ap_20131124_evangelii -gaudium.html.

————. Message for the Celebration of the World Day of Peace. January 1, 2014. http://w2.vatican.va/content/francesco/en/messages/peace /documents/papa-francesco_20131208_messaggio-xlvii-giornata -mondiale-pace-2014.html.

————. Address to the Pentecost Vigil with the Ecclesial Movements. Rome: May 18, 2013. http://w2.vatican.va/content/francesco/en/speeches /2013/may/documents/papa-francesco_20130518_veglia-pentecoste .html.

Gallagher, Timothy M. *The Discernment of Spirits: An Ignatian Guide for Everyday Living*. New York: Crossroad, 2005.

Hart, Anne. "The Friday Everything Changed." In *Inside Stories*, edited by Glen Kirkland and Richard Davies, 2–11. Don Mills, Ontario: Harcourt Brace Jovanovich Canada, 1987.

John Paul II, Pope. Mission of the Redeemer (*Redemptoris Missio*). Encyclical on the Permanent Validity of the Church's Missionary Mandate. December 7, 1990. http://w2.vatican.va/content/john-paul-ii/en /encyclicals/documents/hf_jp-ii_enc_07121990_redemptoris-missio .html.

Knowles, Malcolm S. *The Adult Learner: A Neglected Species.* Fourth edition. Houston, TX: Gulf, 1990.

———. *Using Learning Contracts.* San Francisco, CA: Jossey-Bass, 1991.

Krisak, Tony. "Longing for an Invitation." Paulist Evangelization Ministries. May 2011. http://www.pemdc.org/freeresources/evangelization -exchange-archives/2011-archives/may-2011/may-2011-evangelization -exchange-krisak/.

Krupp, Laure. "Feedback without Fallout." *Eucharistic Ministries* (July 2004): 6.

Maslow, Abraham H. "A Theory of Human Motivation." *Psychological Review* 50.4 (1943): 370–96.

Maslow, Abraham H., and Edward Hoffman. *Future Visions: The Unpublished Papers of Abraham Maslow.* Thousand Oaks: SAGE, 1996.

Palmer, Parker J. *The Courage to Teach: Exploring the Inner Landscape of a Teacher's Life.* Tenth Anniversary ed. San Francisco, CA: Jossey-Bass, 2007.

Paul VI, Pope. On Evangelization in the Modern World (*Evangelii Nuntiandi*). Apostolic Exhortation. December 8, 1975. http://w2.vatican.va/content /paul-vi/en/apost_exhortations/documents/hf_p-vi_exh_19751208 _evangelii-nuntiandi.html.

*Rite of Christian Initiation of Adults.* Ottawa: Canadian Conference of Catholic Bishops, 1987. Print.

*Rite of Christian Initiation of Adults.* Study ed. Collegeville, MN: Liturgical Press, 1988. Print.

Rolheiser, Ronald. *The Holy Longing: The Search for a Christian Spirituality.* Reissue ed. New York: Image, 2009.

Schmidt, Eric, and Jonathan Rosenberg. *How Google Works.* London: John Murray, 2015.

Spadaro, Antonio, SJ. "A Big Heart Open to God: An Interview with Pope Francis." *America.* September 30, 2013. http://www.americamagazine .org/faith/2013/09/30/big-heart-open-god-interview-pope-francis.

Vatican II Council. Constitution on the Sacred Liturgy (*Sacrosanctum Concilium*). December 4, 1963. http://www.vatican.va/archive/hist_councils /ii_vatican_council/documents/vat-ii_const_19631204_sacrosanctum -concilium_en.html.